Jacov Marin

QUEEN OF PEACE
IN MEDJUGORJE

APPARITIONS - EVENTS - MESSAGES

Original translation and editing from Croatian text by:
The Sarcevic Family
MIR Center
Clarks Summit, PA 18411

Edited and Published by:
THE RIEHLE FOUNDATION
P.O. Box 7
Milford, Ohio 45150

In accordance with the decree of Pope Urban VIII and the regulations of the Second Vatican Council, the author states that he does not wish to precede the judgment of the Church to which he completely submits. The words "apparitions, messages, miracles" and similar words, carry here the value of human witnessing.

According to the newest decree of the Vatican, March 7, 1975, (Decree over printed material), "Imprimatur" is no longer binding for all books excluding Holy Scripture, Liturgical books, and handbooks for religious teaching.

Published by The Riehle Foundation
For additional copies, write:
The Riehle Foundation
P.O. Box 7
Milford, Ohio 45150

Copyright 1989 The Riehle Foundation

Library of Congress Catalog Card No.: 89-061648

ISBN: 1-877678-01-5

This book originally published as "KRALJICA MIRA U MEDU-GORJU" in 1988

Published by: Roman-Catholic Parish of St. Mary
Dolac, Kaptol 3, Zagreb, Yugoslavia

Printed by: RO "Informator" OOUR Printery "Zagreb,"
Zagreb, Preradoviceva 21-23, Yugoslavia

TABLE OF CONTENTS

iii

PART THREE

Mother and Educator

Feast of the Exultation of the Cross.

FOREWORD

Many pilgrims and parishioners are mistaken when they think that Medjugorje will become such as Lourdes or Fatima. Medjugorje is neither Lourdes nor Fatima. With Medjugorje, a new era will begin.

Medjugorje does not call you because it is one of the shrines, but because it wishes to lead you toward new times. You have been called here so that your heart opens up completely with love and that this heart be prepared for the events that are to follow, not only here, but in all the world. The messages and secrets of which the visionaries speak concern all of mankind.

Therefore, our hearts must be shaken today. They must be shaken so that Mary's and God's peace enters into them, so that Mary's and God's joy enter into them, and so that we carry that peace and joy into our families, so that they become a new source of peace for others. If we carry this peace in all directions, if this earth begins now to be shaken by the peace, then we can feel good and wonderful on this earth.

Therefore, do not talk too much about Medjugorje, but try to make people understand each other so that peace and joy enter into them. This will all be easy if here you fill yourself with peace and joy; if you decide, from today on, to carry joy and peace.

Full of peace and joy, let us hurry to meet the events, not as those who frighten people with tomorrow, but as those who are happy about meeting with the Heavenly Father and Jesus Christ. Let us begin with a new time in our life, a new time for our families, for this parish and for all of mankind.

May the Queen of Peace pour her peace into our hearts, and through every pilgrim, may the peace start flowing throughout the whole world.

(These are thoughts from the sermon of Tomislav Vlasic in Medjugorje, June 25, 1986, on the fifth anniversary of the apparition.)

Multitude in St. James Church at Medjugorje.

Vicka, Jakov, Maria.

Place of the first apparitions.

Maria and Jakov during an apparition.   *Path up Mt. Krizevac.*

The crowd during the anniversary celebration.

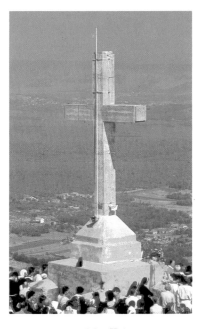

The Cross on Mt. Krizevac.

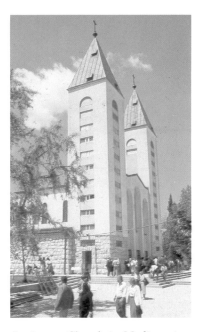

St. James Church in Medjugorje.

Place of first apparitions.
Mt. Krizevac in background.

Maria with Sr. Janja.

*The crowd for the Mass
at St. James Church.*

*The Way of the Cross
on the path up Mt. Krizevac.*

Jelena Vasilj in 1983.

Vicka, Jakov, Ivanka, Maria and Ivan during an apparition.

Confessions in Medjugorje.

Maria meeting pilgrims.   *Pilgrims and reconciliation.*

Con-celebration of the Mass at St. James Church.

Medjugorje—between the mountains.

PART ONE

OUR LADY APPEARS

The First Year

MEDJUGORJE

Until recently, Medjugorje was an unknown village lost in Hercegovina's rocky soil, unknown even in its homeland. Today it is an image. News of it spread not only over our entire homeland, but, in fact, throughout the whole world. It is talked of on all five continents and compared with world renowned places of other Marian apparitions, such as Lourdes and Fatima, which are the destinations of countless pilgrimages from the whole world.

Medjugorje is a village and a parish in the midst of the formation of mountains of Hercegovina on the extreme south of our homeland. Its very name indicates that it is located among mountains. It is the western part of Hercegovina, south-southeast of Mostar, and its distance from Mostar is somewhat less than 30 kilometers.

The road from Mostar runs through Citluk, the county seat, and continues toward Ljubuski. About three kilometers past Citluk the road branches off to the left onto an asphalt road toward Medjugorje, which is located about two kilometers further.

This area looks like a plateau, (though it is not level) and mostly rocky and stony, covered by scant vegetation. Bigger trees are rare and few. The very land around the parish church is a pleasant and fruitful flat ground, all carefully cultivated. The main crops are grapes and tobacco planted on fields which are often fenced in by the stones taken out of the ground and placed around in a border. It is customary here in all rocky areas. There is little rain and few springs or wells can be found. The people gather rain water in cisterns or water-tanks for themselves, for their cattle, and use it for watering the tobacco that needs to be watered immediately after planting.

The parish of Medjugorje had been mentioned in the year 1599. During the Turkish occupation it perished, as did all other parishes in Hercegovina. When the first parishes were restored in the 18th century, Medjugorje became a part of the parish Brotnjo, which later got the name Gradnići in Britnjo. The parish of Medjugorje was established again in the year 1892 and entrusted to the Franciscans of Hercegovina. The old parish church was built in 1897 on soft, unsafe ground and soon could not be used anymore.

Even before the last war, the parishioners were thinking about a new church. Plans were made, enough material was obtained and the building had begun, but, during the war, everything was destroyed except a few partially built walls. After the war, people began to work again and, in 1969, a new, big and spacious church with three knaves and two towers was, for the most part, completed. It was consecrated to St. James, the elder. With its two towers and whiteness, the church stands out beautifully over the entire plain.

At about the same time, three more churches were built in the neighboring villages. Only the village of Bijakovici does not have its own church. The old church was actually situated in Bijakovici, at the very edge of the village. The new one, 200 yards away, is already in Medjugorje. The old church has been demolished, the ruins removed, and the ground now serves as a parking lot. The parish rectory is located between the new church and the place where the old church had been situated, but it is too small and inadequate, especially for the great needs of the present time.

The largest portion of the village of Medjugorje lies some distance from the church, at the foot of the hill, Krizevac, which, until fifty years ago was called Sipovac. The air-line distance from the top of the hill to the parish church is somewhat more than one and a half kilometers. At the top of the hill the parishoners built a high concrete cross in the year 1933, in commemoration of 1900 years of the passion and death of Jesus. There is a beautiful view of the cross from the parish church. The villagers carried all the necessary materials for the cross on their shoulders because there is no road to the top of the hill. The way up the hill was just a narrow goat-path. A simple Way of the Cross has been erected along that route.

The cross stands on the right edge of the hill's peak, when being viewed from the parish church. The hill stretches quite a distance toward the east. A little farther east, to the left of the church, the hill, Crnica, which is somewhat lower than Krizevac, branches off into an arch. A little farther to the left and on the way to the church the village of Bijakovici is located. The portion of the village is directly under the hill called Podbrdo. That name has become common to the part of the hill above the village as well.

It was on the hill, Crnica or Podbrdo, a short distance from the village and a few hundred meters above the village, where the apparitions of the Blessed Mother of God began, which made Bijakovici and Medjugorje famous throughout the world.

The geographical location of the place of apparition is very significant. It is a socialist country, yet almost at the border and not far from the sea, across which is the "capitalist" world. For hundreds of years the Turks occupied, governed and plundered land. They left permanent traces. A mixture of races and religions now lives there: Catholics, Moslems and Eastern-Orthodox, Croats and Serbs.

In a political sense, the East and West are touching here. Many people in this region travel to find work in Western Europe, and many tourists from Western Europe come to this region. In a religious sense, the East, the West and the Orient meet here: Orthodoxy, Catholicism and Islam.

This fact alone says much. It seems that Our Lady could not find a more appropriate place from which to send us her message, especially the message of forgiveness and reconciliation in which she stresses that all, Catholics, Orthodox and Moslems, are her children. Just this repeated emphasis on reconciliation on all levels is, perhaps, the greatest proof of authenticity of the apparitions.

When we speak of the mixture of nations and religions, it concerns a larger area. The immediate area, to the West of the Neretva, Western Hercegovina, represents the purest Croatian region. Only recently have some members of other nations and religions settled there, but they are an insignificant minority. Concerning religion, people in Western Hercegovina are probably the most loyal of all Croatians to their religion. From ancient times, Hercegovina's Franciscans serve in all the parishes in this region. They are commonly called "friars," and have several monasteries here. Their pastoral work has contributed greatly to the fact that the people have retained their religion in such a way and still live by it today.

EVENTS BEFORE THE APPARITIONS

The German priest, Heribert Muhlen, the head of the charismatic movement in Germany, held a lecture in Zagreb a few years ago. At that time he said to the Croatian priests and others in the audience, "God is preparing great things in your homeland, which will greatly influence the destiny of all of Europe." (I am quoting from memory according to one who was present.) Was he truly a prophet?

At the beginning of June, 1981, about three weeks before the first apparition of Our Lady in Medjugorje, there was a Congress of Charismatics held in Rome at which about 700 members of that great church movement from the whole world were present. Among them was a group from our homeland, Croatia. Among them was Fr. Tomislav Vlasic, who was pastor in Caplinja at that time and who was supposed to come, within two months, to Medjugorje. P. E. Tardif, a priest from Central America, who has a special gift of healing from God and who is known to have healed many sick people, prayed over Fr. Tomislav Vlasic for the Church in our country. He then said to him, "Do not be afraid. I am sending you my Mother."

Approximately two months before the apparition, Vicka and her sisters went with a little wagon to gather branches. When they returned to the wagon, they found in the toolbox two big, old-fashioned rosaries of different sizes and forms. On one, the crucifix was almost ten centimeters long and on it were all fourteen Stations of the Cross. There was no one nearby who could have put them there, and they certainly were not there before. Later, during an apparition, Vicka asked Our Lady about these rosaries. She answered that they are her present to Vicka to encourage her to pray.

On the wall of the choir loft, above the front door of the church in Medjugorje, hangs a painted picture. It shows Our Lady in a white dress with a blue belt, white veil and blue cape, as she hovers with outstretched arms above Medjugorje. Below Our Lady in the picture, one can see the hill, Krizevac. At the bottom, on the left side of the picture, there is the parish church of Medjugorje and next to it, trees that grow in front of the church and to the right of the church. The picture was painted in 1974 long before any apparition, by a naive, self-educated painter from Medjugorje, Vlado Falak. Is that picture a prophecy, too?

OUR LADY APPEARS

Wednesday, June 24, 1981. It is a "holy day". Nobody works, because the people still celebrate the Feast of St. John the Baptist as an obligatory holy day. Two high school girls, Ivanka, who lives in Bijakovici, and Mirjana, who was spending her vacation with relatives, went for a walk along the bottom of the hill. It was late afternoon. They walked slowly and talked. Ivanka accidently glanced up the hill and saw something shiny. She looked again and saw, a little farther up the hill, an unusual apparition hovering above the ground. "Look, Our Lady on the hill!"

Mirjana, who says herself that she never in her life dreamed of something like that, answered, "It would be better that you just keep quiet so that nobody hears what you are saying. How could Our Lady appear to us?" And both of them went home.

A little later, Maria's younger sister, Milka, asked the two girls to go with her to look for her sheep. They went the same way passing the foot of the hill. Ivanka again turned and looked up from the foot of the hill. "There she is again—Our Lady!" And she pointed persistently with her finger up the hill.

Then Mirjana and Milka, to their surprise, also saw the apparition a little higher up the hill, holding in her arms something that looked like a child. All three girls remained speechless.

A friend, Vicka came along on the road and they called her to come. All three were very excited and called her loudly. She asked "What is it? Is it a snake?" They called, "It's not a snake!" Vicka came running and when she saw the apparition, she was so scared that she took off her shoes and, in her stocking feet, ran to the village. However, she returned after two or three minutes. She realized she had nothing to fear; it was Our Lady.

She returned with Ivan Dragicevic. In his hands, he was carrying a bag of apples. The girls pointed at the apparition which he, too, could see. But he became so frightened that everything fell from his hands and he ran away and did not come back. With him had been another young man, also named Ivan. He did not return anymore during the later apparitions, stating he thought he was too old for such things.

The girls were very excited when they returned home and could not hide their excitement. Everybody to whom they spoke of the apparition made fun of them and told them to dismiss it.

THE FIRST TALK WITH OUR LADY

The following day, Thursday, the 25th of June, in the evening, the girls went again, at 6:30 p.m. (about the same time as the day before), to the same place. No one had said anything to them, but something pulled them to go there. With them, also, was a woman with a child. Mirjana and Ivanka, along with Vicka and Ivan, also called Jakov and Maria to go, wondering if they too might see something. They called them because they were the only ones who believed their story. The woman present, saw Our Lady and said, "She is extending her arms toward you. Run up the hill." The girls, too, saw the apparition extending her arms as if she were calling them to her. Ivanka & Mirjana ran up the hill, followed by Maria, Jakov, Vicka and Ivan. Some people from the village followed them as well. They also saw something shiny. Milka was not home that day, so it was her sister Maria who came and who remained among the seers. After that, Milka never saw anything further.

The children came before Our Lady and immediately fell to their knees and began to pray. All cried from the excitement. Ivanka's mother had died two months ago, so she asked Our Lady how her mother was. Our Lady answered that she is well, that Ivanka should not worry about her because she is her heavenly angel. They also asked Our Lady whether she would come again tomorrow. And the answer was, *Yes!* The villagers who were present could see that the children were saying something, that they moved their lips, but there was no sound. In parting, Our Lady said, *Go in Peace.* There was suddenly a bright light in the sky, noticed also by those who were present.

THE THIRD APPARITION OF OUR LADY

The third day—a Friday, many people had already gathered there. The children walked again along the road until they saw something. The sky lit up three times. The light fell onto the other side of the hill. At the spot where Our Lady had appeared the day before was a narrow path and it was relatively easy to climb it. But on this side of the hill, there were only rocks, holes, bushes and "weeds" with impassable thorns. It was difficult to pass through. They started to run up the rocks and brush toward the light. Witnesses tell us that the children ran over the rocks, bushes and thorns as if they had wings, to reach Our Lady at a spot which is otherwise difficult to reach. Nobody was hurt, even though the bushes, thorns and rocks are usually impassable. This alone seemed to everyone as a miracle.

So, the children reached Our Lady quickly. Mirjana and Ivanka fainted for a short time from exhaustion and excitement. Vicka sprinkled Our Lady with holy water and salt and said, "In the name of the Father and the Son and the Holy Spirit! If you are the Mother of God, stay; if you are not, go away!" But Our Lady only smiled. Then Mirjana asked for her deceased grandfather whom she liked very much. Ivanka inquired again about her mother.

"Did my mother say anything?" *She is well. She said you should listen to your grandmother, because she is old and you should help her.*

The children also asked Our Lady why she is coming here, and why to them? "We are like anyone else, nothing special." And Our Lady replied that she never seeks only the best. She appeared there because she wants to be among believers. And she turned around and looked at each one of the believers separately. She states she wants all people to be converted. The children also asked Our Lady for a sign so that the people would not ridicule them.

After the apparition on that day, the seer, Maria, rushed home, while the other seers stayed behind. When she came to the small valley called Lokvetina, something pulled her to the side. There Our Lady again appeared to her. But she was very sad: behind her was a big, dark cross. Our Lady cried and said, *Peace, peace, peace and only peace.* Then, through tears, she repeated twice, *There should be more peace between God and mankind, and among people, as well.* Our Lady prayed and Maria prayed with her. After some time, Our Lady disappeared again.

The other seers came by and thought that Maria was ill, but she could not tell them anything. They took her by the hands and took her home. Only then did she tell them what had happened to her. Maria says, "This was a special day for me which will not be easy to forget. That was also the day when the Mother of God, for the first time, prayed for peace."

"On that day, Our Lady really relayed to mankind what is of utmost importance in her message. . .all that Our Lady wanted to tell us by coming among us. And everything else, such as prayer, fasting and penance, are only the means to this peace." (J. Bubalo: *A Thousand Meetings with Our Lady,* page 60-61.)

FURTHER APPARITIONS OF OUR LADY

The next day, Saturday, Ivanka asked, "My Lady, what is your name?"

I am the Blessed Virgin Mary.

Mirjana: "People tell us that we are drug users, epileptics."

My children, there is always injustice in the world, and now, too. Do not pay attention to it.

On Sunday, there was already such a crowd that few could remember a time when so many people were seen in Hercegovina at a religious meeting.

Mirjana: "We had just asked her to leave some kind of sign for the people, but she just turned, looked at the people and smiled."

During the apparition, Our Lady hovers about 30 centimeters above the ground. She always stands on a small cloud. She is very beautiful, slim and about 160 centimeters tall. In his childish frankness, Jakov said, "I have never seen such a beautiful woman!" She wears a long gray dress that covers her feet. Actually, that color is hard to describe. It is gray, and, then again, it seems not to be gray, but some other, indescribable color. On her head is a white veil which hangs to the ground. On her head she wears a crown, shiny as if it were made of stars. She has blue eyes, black eyelashes, small red lips, rosy cheeks, locks of black hair can be seen from under the veil. She is young; about twenty years old. She is so beautiful that we could always simply look at her. She speaks with a gentle voice of normal strength, the tone of which cannot be described. It is like music or singing or the ringing of bells."

Somebody asked the seers, "In what language does Our Lady speak?" "Croatian, of course." Only, the seers say, she does not talk like we do, in a dialect, but in the beautiful, pure Croatian language.

"It is an indescribable joy to see her," says Mirjana.

Jakov: "If I died now, I would not be sorry because I saw Our Lady."

Mirjana: "And then there is that wishful, impatient expectation. We count the minutes and always look at the clock to see if it is time to start praying. And afraid that perhaps we did something and she would not come. It is a great joy and happiness when we see her. When I am next to her, I could cry from happiness."

Before the apparition, Mirjana's grandmother advised the children that they should pray seven Our Father's, Hail Mary's and Glory Be's. This they did and when they finished praying, Our Lady appeared. From then on, they always pray those prayers until Our Lady comes.

From the very beginning, many made fun of them. They mockingly called the girls, "little ladies." They were sad about it and, therefore, asked Our Lady for a sign, so that all would believe them. But after a few days, they did not pay any attention to the ridiculing.

They begged Our Lady to show herself to all the people, so that all could see her. She said only, *Blessed are those who do not see but believe.* And she turned and looked at the people, *They should believe as if they see me.*

AND THE PASTOR WAS NOT HOME...

Fr. Jozo Zovko came to Medjugorje as a pastor at the end of October, 1980, only eight months before the apparition. This change was very difficult for him. He, himself, says that he could not forget his previous parish, Posusje, in northwestern Hercegovina, north of Imotski, and he says that he felt like those Israelites who were sorry to leave Egypt. With difficulty, he accepted God's plan and began his work in the new parish.

Looking from the standpoint of a priest who knows the pastoral situations in our land, Medjugorje would still be considered a very good parish. But Fr. Jozo felt all the shortcomings of his new parish: poor sacramental life, inadequate family prayer, and superfluous traditionalism in the entire Christian life. He tried to do everything he could with the youth, the parents, the members of the Third Order of St. Francis, but he had the feeling that they did not understand him. They complained that he asked of them what others did not ask. Fasting and penance were "hard talk," even for the members of the Third Order of St. Francis, and they reacted openly. More or less, everyone ate meat on Friday, except in Lent, because "the Church had allowed it." Everyone lacked feeling for the Universal Church and her intentions and needs, and, just as much, they lacked a responsibility to the Church. He felt that he was far away from them, but he certainly wanted to persevere to the end.

From June 17 to 24, 1981, Fr. Jozo was leading a retreat for the sisters in Klostar Ivanic in northern Croatia, about 40 kilometers southeast of Zagreb. He recommended his wish and his intention to the sisters' prayers. His intention was that the Lord, with the help of His Spirit, would move his parish. The sisters accepted his intention and prayed for it.

He tried several times to telephone his assistant in Medjugorje, Fr. Zrinko Cuvalo, but could not get the connection. Only after the retreat, he came to Zagreb and learned that lightning had struck the utilities building in Medjugorje. It had burned down completely, together with the post-office and a disco-club that were in it. That was the reason he could not complete his phone call.

Fr. Jozo arrived late at night from Zagreb to his previous parish, in Posusje. There he learned all about the fire but nothing about the apparitions of Our Lady because the Franciscans there did not know anything about them. The next day, on Saturday, June 27, he, along with another brother, visited his mother who was in the hospital in Mostar. After that, he saw in front of the hospital, the car of the "Health Home" in Citluk and in the car, a woman with bandaged hands and feet. That woman immediately asked, "Where is Zrinko? What happened to him?" (He thought something had happened to his assistant.)—"Our Lady is appearing in Medjugorje and he is not there!" Fr. Jozo knew the woman, who was from Bijakovici, but did not take her words seriously.

When he arrived home in Medjugorje, he learned from a nun that the woman in Mostar was right: "Six children are saying that Our Lady is appearing to them. People are gathering at the place of the apparitions. They are coming from all of Brotnjo and Ljubuska Krajina. The parish yard, the space around the church and the road are all full of cars and a great crowd of people."

THE PASTOR QUESTIONS THE CHILDREN

Fr. Zrinko had already spoken with the children and taped the conversation, but for Fr. Jozo, that conversation was no help in learning more. Fr. Zrinko brought out a suspicion which some other people also had, that Mirjana probably brought some drugs from Sarajevo. Some children allegedly saw some of the seers smoking on the hill above the houses and they thought that they had perhaps smoked drugs. Fr. Jozo wanted to talk to the children, but Fr. Zrinko did not want to go to the village alone and they went by car together. On the way, they met a pick-up truck with all the seers, who were on the way to him.

Fr. Jozo did not personally know any one of them. Only Vicka was his pupil in his catechism class, but he did not specifically remember her. Nor, did he know their families before the apparition. None of the seers were ever present at the prayer meeting with Fr. Jozo or with anybody else. Therefore, there is no foundation for the statements of some, who do not want to acknowledge the apparitions, that they are allegedly the fruit of a previous activity of Fr. Zovko in that field.

In the beginning, questioning the children was very difficult. Right away the pastor questioned them individually and taped everything.

He spoke first with Mirjana and let her talk in detail about herself, about her life and her family in Sarajevo. This intelligent high school girl did not let him confuse her. The conversation continued spontaneously and convincingly.

After only a few minutes of conversation with Mirjana he had to conclude that the thought of any use and influence of drugs by the seers must be eliminated, but there remained other doubts.

He was afraid that it may be someone's trick; that someone persuaded the children to do this to fool the people and to discredit him in the parish. Because he did not know either the children or their parents, he did not know what and how much he could believe from them. In addition, there was always the possibility that the devil could cause something like this, with the purpose, of course, to cause damage to faith and to the Church. After he finished questioning all the children, they went home and promised to come in the evening after the apparition.

For the pastor, Fr. Jozo, those were difficult moments and a painful ordeal. He felt the large responsibility that lay upon him.

That afternoon, cars blocked the road. People rushed toward the hill. A big group could already be seen on the hill, among the thorns. The assistant pastor and another Franciscan went too, but in civilian clothes. Fr. Jozo did not go. From the shadow of a big cypress tree he observed the hill on which poured great streams of people from all sides. Everyone wanted to be as close as possible to the seers. Evidently, only pure curiosity prompted them. Everyone expected to see and experience something unusual. When they returned from the hill, one could hear quite a bit of cursing from the people, disillusioned that they did not see anything of what they had expected. There were also quite a few priests who had climbed the hill and on their return, they visited the pastor, enthusiastic about the fact that so many people seek "signs and miracles." But nor were the priests truly satisfied and happy. Here, as well, there was too much curiosity, doubt and emotion.

After Fr. Jozo questioned the seers the first time, in the afternoon of the same day, officials from the secret police (the SUP) came and took the children to Citluk where they questioned them. Later, they took them to see physicians, also in Citluk. After that, the children returned home by taxi cab so that they could be on time on the hill, where they again experienced their meeting with Our Lady. Only Ivan stayed back in Citluk, and so did not get back on time to the hill. He experienced the apparition somewhere in the village, when he was on the way to the hill.

SUNDAY, JUNE 28, 1981

On Saturday evening, after a talk with the children, Fr. Jozo stayed alone with his assistant. He did not sleep, but listened again to the tape of the conversation with the children. He fell asleep after ardent prayer. On Sunday morning, he was awakened by the noises of pilgrims. He decided to remain in the parish church and send his assistant to celebrate Mass out in the chapels. In his sermon, he discussed a general view of revelation through history, starting with Abraham. He felt that the people listened much more attentively than usual.

He stressed the greatness of the Church as the heir of Revelation and of all the promises of God. He emphasized that the life of Christians draws its strength from the Sacraments and the Bible. Our unavoidable call is to convert and believe in the Scriptures. He did not mention the apparitions on Crnica, but talked about Lourdes, Fatima and other apparitions of Our Lady. He stressed that this was the call of Heaven to man who forgot the Divine values, his dignity, and basic duties in a specific time. The tragedy of present-day man is the fact that he has conformed with those who abandoned the well of living water, and built for themselves a tank that cannot hold water. . .

In talking with the people after Holy Mass, he was very careful. He wished to learn from them some details about the seers and their parents, but the answers were miserly and ordinary. At the Masses he announced an afternoon prayer and meditation, with an already formed group of young boys and girls in the parish, and he also invited others to come to the church to pray—"whoever wants to come, to pray together for the grace to see and distinguish whether or not

God is at work here." After the Mass, he again questioned the children-seers.

That afternoon about thirty young people came. They prayed together, feeling that their faith was being tested and with the intention that God should show them the way, and not to fall, and that God's will be done. After the prayer, the pastor asked them: "What do you think; do the children deceive us?"

A girl mentioned that the sister of Vicka, Ana, who is older than Vicka, was present. She had finished medical school.

"What do you think, Ana, do the children deceive us; does Vicka cheat us? You know her!"

The girl was evidently hurt by the question. She became very upset and began to cry: "I know my sister; she does not lie!"

Only later she explained that she had always (prior to the apparition), seen a light which announced the coming of Our Lady and, therefore, the question was terrible for her.

The pastor did not question them further, but he suggested praying the rosary in order that they might realize what it is that God wanted from them in that moment. Was God at work here or not? A great multitude of people were already on the hill, but there were enough people gathered in the church, as well. Fr. Jozo gave a long meditation on the rosary. They tried to pray piously, open to God's will.

After the rosary, all went up the hill and the pastor remained alone, in prayer. At that time, he had already begun to abandon the doubt that the apparitions could be somebody's trick, but he still had one more problem.

"If the children lied in the beginning, it is now hard for them to admit it. Perhaps they want to be stubborn. But this must soon show itself because the children cannot persevere for a long time."

That doubt was slowly being rejected, just as the doubt about the drugs which seemed to him the hardest. Not long ago, he wrote a few articles for *Nasa Ognjista* ("Our Hearts") and he saw before him all that he had read about it, and was afraid that perhaps drugs had found their way into his parish.

The next day was the holyday of St. Peter and Paul, June 29. The seers were ready to go to Holy Mass, when officials from Citluk came and took them, accompanied by their parents or a relative, for a psychiatry examination in Mostar. That evening, all were back again on the hill and, surrounded by a multitude, experienced the apparition of Our Lady.

APPARITION AT CERNO

On Tuesday, June 30, in the afternoon, two women took the seers for a ride in a car through Hercegovina. All went, except Ivan, who did not want to go. It was arranged very cleverly, so that the seers would not realize what was going on. Officials definitely wanted to check to see if the children would have the same experience away from the hill.

They took them through Zitomislic, Pocitelj, Capljina, Kravica and Cerno. On the way they gave them various treats.

Returning on the road between Ljubuski and Medjugorje, they reached Cerno about 6 o'clock in the evening. They turned from the main road to a place from which the Bijakovici hill could be seen. At that moment, all the children cried: "Stop!" They stopped the car by the road, all came out of the car, and the five seers immediately knelt down and started to pray. One of the women wanted to light a cigarette. All of a sudden, there was a pillar of light in front of them, which overflowed them. The children experienced the apparition, their meeting with Our Lady, just as on previous days on the hill. The women were shocked, the cigarette fell from the hand. It seemed to them that the sun and the light would fall upon them. Both had seen the same event and felt the same fear. After the apparition the women managed to bring the children to the church in Medjugorje, and then, still excited, they looked for the pastor to tell him what they had seen and experienced.

The officials from the secret police also questioned the Franciscans from Medjugorje, the parents of the children, and many villagers. They suspected that Mirjana brought drugs from Sarajevo, and that the children have visions under such influence. But all their investigations in that direction brought no results. The physicians' reports from Citluk and Mostar also rejected any possibility of the use of drugs or any influence of any psychological illness. The doctors proclaimed the children completely healthy and normal.

The whole parish was now in trouble, together with the pastor and the Franciscans. Friars came every day, from the whole region, in civilian clothes, and stated their doubts, observations, thoughts and suggestions. They suggested all kinds of things: to go to the hill and there to pray the rosary with the people, even to build an altar on the hill.

But God evidently had His plans, and everything worked to realize those plans. The pastor faced the biggest problem. Everybody else went home, got busy with other things, and for the moment forgot their common trouble. Only the pastor had to remain alone, solve everything alone, and persevere in faith and trust in God.

On Wednesday, July 1, in the afternoon, Fr. Jozo was alone in the church, kneeling in the pew and praying. Actually, he was there every afternoon, alone, and praying while the people rushed by the church to the hill, urged by curiosity. All this curiosity and wishing for sensation, bothered and offended his soul very much, especially when he heard people swearing when they returned from the hill. He did not feel the necessity to go there himself. He was alone in the church. He prayed and meditated, prayed the psalms from the breviary, sifting his soul for some events in the history of our redemption. He remembered the troubles of Abraham, Moses...

"My God, this multitude of people gathers here, amasses here in my parish. I feel it as a big ordeal. What do I have to do?" He was afraid that perhaps Satan was using this, that the enemies of the religion were using it. "God, if you wish something from these people, if you wish something from me, I am ready, tell me!"

And he prayed in this way, truly praying with his whole heart, aware of his responsibility before God, before his conscience, before the whole church. He felt that he must be there and pray and wait for a sign from God to show him

what to do—he suddenly heard a voice very clearly, as if someone were standing right next to him saying: "Go out now
and protect the children!"

He immediately stood up from the pew and headed out of
the church through the center door. As he took hold of the
doorknob and was opening the door, and just as he took one
step out, all of a sudden the children-seers, all six of them,
pasted themselves to him like a swarm of bees: "The police
are after us, hide us!"

He hurried the children to the rectory, unlocked the doors
and hid the children in an empty room which no one used.
"Stay here, calm down and keep quiet!" He had just come
out of the house and saw three militia men running by the
church. They stopped and asked him: "Did you see the children?" "I did!" Then they kept on running toward Bijakovici,
and the children remained in the house. The police had started
chasing them when they had planned to go on up the hill,
but they slipped away and ran below the village, through the
vineyards, below the graveyard, and ran up to the church from
the west side. As they were squeezing through the vineyards,
under the taut wires upon which the grapevines climb, the
militia couldn't keep up, and so they got away.

That evening the children had—for the first time—the vision in the parish house. Because of some difficulties they
could not go to the hill. The pastor was not present.

The days of the first week of the apparitions are loaded
with events which certainly occurred, but today it is not possible to determine their exact order, because nobody recorded
the events and this would be the only reliable source.

TRANSFER TO THE CHURCH

During the first days, Fr. Jozo said on one occasion to the
children: "Children, ask a favor of Our Lady. Ask her if she
could appear in the church? On the top of the hill, among
the thorns, it is not possible to organize what Our Lady wishes,
a program for conversion, fasting, penance and prayer. Up there
the Holy Mass could not be celebrated or a sermon given or

confession held. This is all possible in the church."

It seems the children asked Our Lady this, at Cerno. Jakov asked her if she would want to appear in the church? And they say Our Lady answered somewhat reluctantly, without enthusiasm, *Yes, I will appear in the church.*

When Our Lady answered, a new problem was created: "Children, how are we going to tell this to the people? People do not want to go to the church, people climb the hill."

And, little Jakov, then still unbelievably small, said: "Well, Fr. Jozo, we did not tell the people to go to the hill. The people are only in our way, we would like it if there were no people around us. It is easier to talk alone to Our Lady. They push us, they push Our Lady, they are stepping on her cape, and Our Lady quickly leaves. But if she wishes that the people come to the church, she will take care of it just as on the hill."

On Thursday, July 2, before the liturgical reform (this was the Feast of Our Lady's Visiting Elizabeth), about 1 o'clock in the afternoon, the yard was already full of people. And the later it became, the more people came. Some went to the hill, others stayed. The ones on the hill, returned again. In the evening, the church and the yard were full. The pastor said a prayer and quickly prepared a sermon.

Before Holy Mass the seers were leading the rosary, kneeling behind the altar. And during the praying of the rosary, Our Lady appeared in the church. She hovered above the people, at the back above the entrance, in front of the choir loft. She appeared above all the people. It seems that the pastor, Fr. Zovko, too, saw Our Lady.

During the Mass he gave a sermon about conversion, about the ways that lead to God, and especially about fasting, penance and prayer. An enormous mass of people listened and absorbed the Word of God. It seemed as if they were hearing it for the first time. It fell like drops of rain on a dry and thirsty ground and created in them new spirit and a new heart.

Carried away and inspired, Fr. Zovko put into the sermon this question:

"Would you accept with love and joy to fast three days on bread and water—that nobody eats anything as a sign of penance and conversion? To reject the power of Satan and the spirit of evil among us?" "We will!" was the thundering answer.

"Will you pray every day in your homes with families?" "We will!" was the answer, so strong that the pastor felt that he would fall over, that the church roof would break. He looked up to the ceiling, but everything was in its place. But something else was breaking and falling in the lives and souls and families of those present. The pastor felt that the great multitude "left Egypt" and started toward the Promised Land.

"Will you every day read the Bible with your families?" "We will!" was the answer, as the final orientation toward God and His Word.

After that, the pastor encouraged those present: "The name of our God is Yahweh, constantly present with us and in us, in life and in work. Unfortunately, we did not recognize Him. This evening He revealed Himself. We recognized Him in this holy community and in the breaking of bread. He put our hearts on fire explaining the Scriptures."

Following the sermon, all solemnly confessed their faith, renounced Satan and renewed their baptismal vows. Afterwards they did that regularly at the beginning of each Mass, after the act of contrition. Fr. Zovko felt the gathered people lacked true faith. True faith must eliminate this great curiosity and wish for sensationalism. It became so moving that the resulting grace was felt and seen. These rites were often interrupted by the loud outcries of individual sinners, renewing their faith, renouncing Satan, and accepting God and loyalty to Him.

After the Mass that day, the seers came to the front of the church, and in front of all the people, publicly and loudly, stated their testimony of how they looked at Our Lady and transmitted her messages. This they did later many more times. Their testimony became much stronger, livelier and more direct than if someone else would have relayed it. Since Jakov was so very small, the pastor had to permit him to climb up on the altar, so that the people could see him when he talked. And that testimony of the children had its own effect. People listened very attentively; the grace of God worked in their souls.

Fr. Jozo finished one Mass with the statement: "Our Lady

is here. You can pray here and make your vows here. Look for her here!"

The people remained long after that, crying and praying. After the seven Our Father's, seven Hail Mary's and seven Glory Be's and the Creed, they prayed, kneeling, still one more rosary. All wanted to pray. Nobody wanted to go home. This lasted until midnight. The pastor then suggested that they continue praying at home and come back tomorrow.

That was the actual moment of conversion of the parish, of all present in the church. That was the first wave of conversion (many others followed), and they have not yet ceased to this day. All fasted for three days. They ate almost nothing. They stopped cooking, they started to pray, to cry, to make sacrifices and to go to Confession. All kept their word, nobody wanting to break his promise. People immediately started to lose the habit of cursing. They talked it over among themselves, and if one should unthinkingly curse, he had to pay a fine. Later they would bring this gathered money to the church.

And so it started.

Yes, this is how the conversion of the whole parish began. Now, all try hard to faithfully accomplish everything Our Lady wishes. Every day the faithful pray 7 Our Father's, 7 Hail Mary's, 7 Glory Be's and the Creed. They pray either at home together, or in the evening in the church, together with the multitude of people, before or after Holy Mass. Every evening, so many come that all could not find room in the church. There they pray the rosary and attend the Mass. The sermons of the priests and the prayers of the faithful in this church seem to be more sincere and more appealing than in other places.

After the 2nd of July, the children saw Our Lady in the choir loft of the church several more times. Later, according to the wish of Our Lady, after the end of the Mass and other prayers, they would go to the hill Crnica and there experience an apparition. When the people learned about that they started to come to the hill in great numbers, forcing the children to meet Our Lady in various places: below the village, in the field, or in the woods. The people began to follow them there, as well, so the children started to meet in the homes of individual seers. Everyone wanted Our Lady to come to his or her house. However, the meetings were most often in the house of the youngest and poorest seer, Jakov, below the village. Several times they experienced the apparition in the rectory. From February of 1982, the apparitions occurred regularly in the small chapel in the parish church next to the altar, across from the sacristy.

THE BLOSSOMING OF RELIGIOUS LIFE

During the summer of 1981 more and more priests had come daily, even from outside of Hercegovina. They helped with confessions and participated in celebrating the Mass. The church was so full that one was unable to move. Holy Communion was therefore distributed after Holy Mass as well. Then followed the prayers of Our Lady's young witnesses, kneeling together with all the people. Later it also included praying the rosary after the Mass. Since many of the sick sought a personal meeting with the young seers, special prayers for seriously ill was also introduced.

Every evening after the Mass and after the seers and the faithful had finished praying, a Franciscan gave the pilgrims a short report on the history of the apparitions and on Our Lady's messages. This was necessary because there were always some people present who had come to Medjugorje for the first time.

The number of penitents who went to Confession, received Holy Communion, and attended Mass grew every day. Confession for many was the first in years. They came by vehicle and on foot. Young people from all regions of Hercegovina came on foot from a distance of 80 to 100 miles. People also came from the farthest parts of our country (Yugoslavia).

Attracted by an inner need, prompted by mental anxiety or physical pain, they found themselves here, together— Catholics, Orthodox, Moslems and others—persons of all occupations and levels. Total goodwill among people, kindness, satisfaction—and all without food, drink and entertainment—such that an objective observer would not find in the best-organized mass gatherings. Unbearable summer heat did not hinder the pilgrims coming to the hill, or to the church, which is very spacious. Around Assumption Day, the number was more than 10,000 and that Saturday and Sunday, 15,000. On the Holy day of the Assumption people who were there believe that there were even over 25,000 pilgrims. Only in the late fall did the number of pilgrims decrease.

Due to the many cars in the summer of 1981, the police kept order. All the vehicles had to stop a kilometer or two from the church, so that around the church there was a beautiful atmosphere of peace and concentration. It was like an environment made to order for a personal meeting with God, in Confession, in prayer and in Communion.

According to incomplete evidence, from the beginning of July to the end of October in 1981 about 200,000 faithful received Holy Communion in Medjugorje. The pilgrims who joined the Medjugorje prayer meetings had, for the most part, carried the fruits of these unique events to their homes. Personal and family prayers were accepted by even those who had neglected them for years. It seems that among the young people, more than among the older ones, there is adherence to fast on bread and water.

In Medjugorje and its surroundings, all (but a few rare exceptions) were fasting, even the children. Lives of the people were showing miraculous transformations. Many were bringing convincing proofs of physical healings by the intercession of Our Lady. During that summer and fall, people in Bijakovici and Medjugorje had given to God and to people, more than ever before, their time, their strength, food, drink, and shelter. They themselves stress that by their generous self-denial, they had received much more than could ever be bought.

A MULTITUDE OF PILGRIMS FROM THE ENTIRE LAND

In the summer and fall of 1981, quite a big number of faithful came from the Orthodox and the Islamic faith to Medjugorje. According to their own statements, both written and oral, those faithful took unforgettable memories with them. They came from very distant places: from Leskovac, Zajecar, Sabac, Smederevo, Belgrade and Subotica. And Moslem pilgrims also came from long distances, such as a group from Zagreb, for example.

In Medjugorje, a new pilgrim center had opened, into which streamed a river of pilgrims. But this center did not offer anything that would divert the pilgrims from the true purpose of their trip. Our Lady's calling for prayer and penance found a full answer from God's people who came there from near and far, often disregarding the very big sacrifices and efforts that this trip entails. Very often they came on foot, even barefoot, from great distances. At least two cases are known of individuals that came on foot from Germany. In Medjugorje people pray long, they pray much, and with an enthusiasm hardly seen anywhere else.

Nobody can say for certain how many pilgrims have visited Medjugorje. Until the end of October 1981, there were certainly over half a million. Some say it was a million. According to the appraisal of the Franciscans of Medjugorje, by the end of 1982, there were one and half million, but these appraisals were certainly low. The real number was certainly much higher. To the end of October 1981 there were at least 100,000 confessions, and some believe there were even up to 150,000 confessions. There were at least 200,000 and perhaps even 300,000 communions. It is impossible to check these numbers. It was certainly a huge multitude.

But most important of all is that the greatest majority of this multitude rushed there on wings of faith and sincere piety. Many who came out of pure curiosity were converted there and completely changed. All visitors talk about a particularly special atmosphere which exists there among the local people. From among pilgrims and priests, both local and those who come from afar, the reaction is the same.

PILGRIMS ON THE HILL OF APPARITIONS

On August 7, 1981, Our Lady called the children to come (at 2 o'clock at night) to the hill and pray there, *because it is necessary to pray for the sinners.* A nun was in Medjugorje from the 10th to the 12th of August. She slept two nights in Maria's house, immediately below the hill of apparitions. She describes:

"I was often awakened at night by the song 'Mary, oh Mary, how beautiful you are. . . ,' or 'Hear us, Mother. . . ,' 'Christ, in Your name,' or other religious songs. I was especially glad to hear young men sing: 'Mother of God, listen to our voice, give us holy priests to lead us to heaven.' All during the night the pilgrims climbed the hill to the place of apparitions."

Until August 12th, the pilgrims very steadily went up the hill and prayed and sang there. On the rocks on the hill there were many inscriptions, prayers, calls and recommendations to Our Lady for sick people. The whole hill was like a pilgrim's church, full of thanksgivings and petitions.

At the place of apparitions on the hill there are two simple wooden crosses one or two meters apart from each other. These crosses indicate the spots above which Our Lady stood during the apparitions. All the apparitions of Our Lady on the hill occurred at these spots, except the third one, which was about 200-300 meters away from the road. At this spot, around and behind the second cross, there is quite a deep recess because the pilgrims dug out the soil and stones, after they had first pulled out all the grass and bushes. These they took with them as a dear souvenir of Our Lady who on these spots, stepped on our land.

The place of apparitions cannot be seen from below, in Bijakovici, but can be seen very clearly from a greater distance, for example, from the church or from the village Medjugorje under the hill Krizevac. It can be seen as a somewhat lighter spot on the dark-green background of the hill. The access to the hill is quite difficult; it is similar to the path which (with the Stations of the Cross), leads up the hill, Krizevac.

On the 12th of August, 1981, at three o'clock in the morning, guards from the civil defense and militia men were placed there and, all the accesses to the hill of apparitions and Krizevac was forbidden.

On August 17, 1981, early in the morning some officials
of the secret police (SUP) arrested the Pastor, Fr. Jozo Zovko
and Fr. Ferdo Vlasic, editor of the magazine, *Our Hearts*
("Nasa Ognjista") who came to help the local priests. It included a search of the parish house and the church which
lasted all day. They took all the money they found, which
was mostly money given for masses, some gifts from the faithful, and money for the household. Later, however, this money
was returned. Both arrested priests were sentenced to a punishment in jail. This was described in *The Voice of the Council*
("Glas Koncila"), No. 18/81 September 13th, 1981.

In an article under the title: "Our Lady with the Little Ones,"
in the paper called *Krsni Zavicaj* No. 20, 1987, Fr. Slavko
Barbaric describes the events of those days. I will quote a
part of this article here which I find necessary (Pg. 242-244):

"Shortly after the beginning of the apparitions, government
officials called the visionaries and their families to a questioning as well as many from the parish community, and they
tried to stop all these happenings by 'convincing' the visionaries to refrain from spreading such stories.

"One physician from Citluk, whose duty was to come and
keep the children in conversation during the apparition, admits in his testimony: 'We spoke with them nicely. There was
no problem. We were in the home of one of the seers. They
were all there. The atmosphere was pleasant, and I was hoping we would continue with the conversation until after the
time of the apparition, and in this way, everything would be
solved. However, when the apparition time came, they all flew
to Podbrdo without stopping. Nothing more could be done.
And I myself ran with the others...'

"The officials wanted the pastor, Fr. Jozo, to discontinue
the evening Mass and to close the church in the afternoon.
He stood before a difficult decision. The church had to be
closed in one way or another. But he did not consent. August
17, 1981 approached. On that day Fr. Jozo Zovko was taken
to prison and, after him, Fr. Ferdo Vlasic. All of the members of the parish household were held and questioned. They
did not know what was happening outside. The church was

closed. The evening Mass should no longer be celebrated—
this was the intent. This would succeed as far as the efforts
of hierarchy were concerned. The pastor was suspended, and
other members of the household were not allowed to leave
the house. However, God's people were coming and, just as
the river Jordan was once blocked, the people just stood before the closed entrances to the church, but stood peacefully
and solemnly. It was at this time that the government officials
decided to open the church, because otherwise the people would
be praying outside of church space.

"The laity, led by the strength of the spirit of prayer, peace
and reconciliation, were not looking for any kind of confron-
tation, but just wanted the church to be opened. One of the
witnesses of this, a priest, testifies the following:

" 'At about 4:30 p.m., I arrived with a number of pilgrims
from Mostar to Medjugorje. One could not go further than
the bridge. The entrance into the village was blocked. Militia
were standing on the bridge as a sign that you could not go
on. They were already all tired out, because they had to keep
answering the same questions to those who came up to them.
They told them that they could not pass, because there would
be no evening Mass, that Fr. Jozo Zovko himself said so. At
this information, no one returned home, but nobody tried to
force his way either. The crowds continued to pour in, just
like a flood, after a continuous downpour. They just stayed there.'

" 'At around 5:00 p.m., which was about the time that praying had normally begun in the church, one of the faithful
present said to Me: 'Father, why not lead us in prayer here
since it seems we can't do so in the church anyway.' I was
aware of the risks of personally beginning prayer there as it
would be looked upon as a rebellion or a stirring up of the
people. But since they had called on me, I conceded and tried
to find a place from which I could lead the prayer. I headed
toward a parked van-and many others followed. As I was about
to begin praying, an applause resounded throughout the crowd,
and these words echoed from mouth to mouth, 'They're let-
ting us in!' All those present and all those who were still
coming at once created a glorious prayerful procession. The
prayers and songs were led by one of the pilgrims with a

beautiful clear voice. There were official guards watching all this from the sides. I found out later that they informed the headquarters that instead of returning home, the people were staying by the bridge and were beginning to pray outside. At this, the chief of police gave orders to allow the people to pass to the church, and enter into it.'

" 'I well recall that peaceful, prayerful walk toward the church, the heartfelt prayers and songs. That pilgrim with the clear voice continued leading the rosary and starting songs. The church was quickly filled. I entered the sacristy and connected a speaker, intending to lead the rosary, but found that it wasn't necessary as the people were already praying and singing in unity.'

" 'Entry into the rectory was impossible. Along with other priests, I was hearing the confessions of those present. When the time for Mass came, I got up and went to the sacristy, intending to celebrate Mass if no one else was there. At that moment, the local Franciscan, Fr. Slavko Dodig, entered the sacristy and told me that he would be saying Mass. He was all dusty and sweaty because he had just come in through the vineyards. He celebrated the Holy Mass, and I led the singing, because those that usually did this, were unable to get to the front.'

" 'There was prayer and song, and there were even tears when it was announced what had happened with the pastor. But the entire people still remained solemn and peaceful.' "

OUR LADY'S MESSAGE

Our Lady very often repeated her call to the people for conversion. She requests live and strong faith, persevering prayer and penance, reconciliation, forgiveness and peace. The seers say that Our Lady requests a general penance and in addition, she stresses fasting. Mirjana transmits her message, word for word:

> *Tell the people I need their prayers, prayers of the whole people, to pray as much as possible and*

*to do penance, because very few nations have con-
verted. There are many Christian nations who still
live like pagans. There are few true believers.*

From various repeated words of Our Lady, it can be concluded that she needs our prayers and penance so that she
could intervene for us before God. In spite of the fact that
many convert in Medjugorje, Our Lady still complains that
few people convert, and repeatedly calls for conversion "while
there is still time."

The seers testify that Our Lady many times expressed her
satisfaction over the people who come to Medjugorje, convert, reconcile, pray and fast.

The Franciscans prepared a short review of events and messages of Our Lady for the pilgrims in Medjugorje. Here are
the most important parts from this review:

Peace and reconciliation. Our Lady wants the people to
reconcile with one another. Evidently, she wants the reconciliation on all lines and levels, from individuals and families,
to big communities, nations and states. In the reconciliation
is also included forgiveness of all injustices and wrongdoings.
In the first days of July, 1981, when Our Lady sent this message, above the hill Krizevac (and the concrete cross on it)—
the word "MIR" ("PEACE")—was written in big fiery letters
in the sky. Many villagers, including their pastor, Fr. Zovko,
saw it. On several occasions, Our Lady talked to the children
about the great tensions in the world among the countries,
and how mankind stands on the brink of a catastrophy—and
she called the world to conversion.

Conversion. Many Christians are registered as Christians,
but never remember their baptism and even less the obligations that follow. Others go to church, but without faith. Christians must be a living sign for others, so that they, too, would
convert and be saved. All must be converted.

Prayer. There are Christians who have completely forgotten
about prayer. It is necessary to return to prayer. Our Lady,
therefore, recommended as a minimum to pray daily, in addition to other prayers, 7 Our Father's, Hail Mary's and Glory
Be's and the Creed. She also said that a needed prayer is

the Creed. It should be prayed as well as lived.

Fasting. Fasting has practically disappeared from Christian practice. It must be renewed. Our Lady called the world to fast. She asked us to fast on Fridays, on bread and water.

Our Lady did not give all these messages at once. From the conversation with the seers, it is evident that they are always present through Our Lady's apparitions in everything she talks about. Peace, conversion and the healing of the sick are all impossible without fasting and prayer, as Our Lady always recommends when somebody asks for counsel in solving a problem, or the grace of healing.

A MESSAGE TO PRIESTS AND RELIGIOUS

When the children asked Our Lady what message she would have for priests and nuns, Our Lady answered: *They should strongly believe and guard the faith of their people!* She sent that message in the first days of July, 1981. Later, when individual priests asked through the children what they should do, in particular, the answers were always: *Perform your duties well and the requests of the Church!* On February 13, 1982, she sent a message to seminarians, the future priests: *Everything is attained with prayer.*

In a letter about her stay in Medjugorje, a nun says: "Talk to everybody and write to everybody. Our fatherland is receiving unspeakable graces through this gift from Heaven. Let us give thanks. I could write innumerable pages about the inner fruits of the meeting with the heavenly Mother, the Queen of Peace."

OUR LADY PRAYS BEFORE
THE CROSS OF HER SON

On December 7, 1981, looking at the people praying, fasting and converting in Medjugorje, Our Lady said: *People convert well, but not all of them. . .* The next day, on the holyday of the Immaculate Conception, the children expected Our Lady to be happy and singing, but she surprised them. When she came, she was very serious, she knelt down with outstretched arms and prayed: *My Son, Whom I love very much, I beg You, forgive the world the grievous sins by which they offended You...* She prayed for some time. The children could not repeat word for word all the words. Then, she prayed together with the children, the Our Father and the Glory Be. And she also said that every day on the hill Krizevac, under the concrete cross, she prays to her Son to forgive the world their sins.

VISIBLE AND MYSTERIOUS SIGNS

Several times, Our Lady has promised a sign, a large, permanent sign. That sign should occur on the hill Crnica, on the place where Our Lady appeared. It will be lasting, tangible, and visible for all. When this large sign comes to pass, it will be accompanied by other miraculous signs and miraculous healings. The sign will be given for those who do not believe in the apparitions of Our Lady. For now, the seers are not permitted to say anything more about it. When asked whether they would be allowed in advance, before the sign occurs, to inform the people about it, they said that they do not know. The sign will occur only after many people convert. In the meantime, there were several other signs, seen by many, local people and pilgrims, priests and nuns.

Most of the signs occur on the hill Krizevac at the big concrete cross. Many have seen how the cross sometimes spins, faster or slower. Actually, it can be seen that the transversal arms of the cross disappear and then again appear, which gives the impression that the cross turns. The cross also sometimes gives off light, while it is turning. That event was always observed from below, from the village of from the church. Everyone who has good eyes can clearly see the cross from below.

More significant are the signs with the white light. The light comes and little by little covers the cross, and in its place, then, the image of Our Lady becomes visible. Or, the image of Our Lady can be seen next to the cross. These signs were seen in several forms and they occurred most often on Friday, but also on other days. The second big sign was mentioned before. It appeared at the beginning of July 1981, above the hill, Krizevac. The word, "MIR" ("PEACE") was written in the sky with big fiery letters. The turning of the cross and the white light and the figure of Our Lady on the place of the cross or next to it, were often seen by hundreds, sometimes thousands of people.

When the seers asked Our Lady what is the meaning of these signs, she answered: *These are advance signs for those who do not believe. The big sign will come later, soon, very quickly.* All the seers know what the sign will be like, but are not allowed to say. All except Maria know, also, when it is going to come, but they cannot relay this either, nor do they talk about it among themselves. Each one keeps for himself what he or she knows.

Sometimes some signs were also seen on Crnica, on the hill of the apparitions. For example, there appeared a big fire on that hill. It could be seen from a good distance. The fire was so big that firemen and militia came to extinguish it, but they did not find a trace of fire.

Many also saw signs in the sun. It is like a repeated miracle of Fatima. (The miracle of the sun in Fatima on October 13, 1917, was seen by about 70,000 persons. Many newspapers reported it. Many persons saw it at a radius of 15 miles. Therefore, mass suggestion was eliminated. The sun started to turn and shine in rainbow colors).

When Our Lady comes to the seers she is most often announced by a light, but she often simply comes without any signs that would announce her. And when she comes, she appears most of the time with a cross, a sun and a heart. When the seers asked her about it, Our Lady, herself, explained that the cross on which her Son was crucified is a symbol of faith. The sun that gives us light is the symbol of God the Father. The heart is a symbol of the love of Our Lady for all of us, especially for the sinners. Ivan, in his diary, mentions only the cross and the heart.

ENTRUSTED SECRETS

Our Lady promised the visionaries that she will reveal ten secrets to each of them. The first three secrets she told them when they were all together. By the beginning of September, 1982, Ivanka received eight secrets all together, and of the remaining visionaries, some had received seven and some received six secrets. On the Feast of the Assumption, 1982, the other seers received the secret which was the eighth one for Ivanka. The secrets deal with future events and can be divided into three groups.

The first group concerns the whole of mankind, the second group concerns the parish of Medjugorje, and the third deals with individual seers. It seems that not all the seers have received the same secrets, but that each one has, in part, his or her own secrets. None of these secrets can be revealed by the seers to anyone, not even to the Holy Father. At the suggestion of the local pastor, the visionaries asked Our Lady whether they could at least reveal the secrets to the church superiors. Our Lady answered that she herself will tell them when, to whom, and how they should reveal the secrets.

There was talk, even reported in some foreign papers, that the seers received an order from Our Lady to reveal the secrets personally to the Holy Father, that they were waiting for the invitation from Rome and that they were happy about the imminent trip. On February 13, 1982, in a conversation with the seminarians, Maria, in the presence of Ivanka, said the following about the secrets: "We have asked whether or not we could speak. She told us that for now, we should not talk, because she will tell us when and give us the time."

Some thought that they could trick little Jakov into revealing the secrets because he was too young to be able to keep quiet; but all the efforts in this direction were not successful in the least.

THE QUEEN OF PEACE

At the end of August 1981, in accordance with the wish of a priest, the visionaries asked Our Lady how else she is called. She answered: *I am the Queen of Peace.* Somewhere around Easter, 1982, one of the seers asked Our Lady during an apparition, whether or not she would like her own special feast day. Our Lady answered that she wishes the 25th of June, the day when she spoke with the children for the first time, be celebrated as the feast day of the Queen of Peace.

It is interesting that June 25th is the day of the third and last apparition of Our Lady in Marienfried, in the parish Pfaffenhofen by Ulm in Germany. (Marienfried means: the Peace of Mary). There were three apparitions altogether: April 25, May 25 and June 25, 1946. The message of Our Lady from Marienfried is very significant, but unfortunately very little known, even in Germany.

THE FRUITS OF THE APPARITIONS

In Medjugorje and Bijakovici no one has any doubts about the apparitions. All the faithful accepted the messages of Our Lady very seriously. Cursing, quarrels and hatred have completely disappeared. As time goes by, among the local people, just as among the pilgrims, there is less and less talk about the apparitions and about miraculous healings, even though there are many of them and everyone believes in them. However, they all live a completely new life. The apparitions of Our Lady brought a basic turnover in the lives of these people, and that change is lasting. All are talking about an inner transformation, reconciliation and forgiveness. The peace of heart which Our Lady promised is visible in these people.

Pilgrims who leave Medjugorje, young and old, ordinary believers, priests, friars and nuns, talk about a tremendous peace in their souls and an inner joy that fills them for days. To many in the parish of Medjugorje it had been difficult to remain in church for just half an hour. Now, it is not difficult for them to remain praying even four hours. After the evening services and devotion, when the priests send them off to go to their homes or lodgings, many people want to stay longer, and some actually stay. All who were there talk about an unusual order and silence in the church. Nobody looks at anybody else, everybody concentrates on his or her prayer. Only those who come out of pure curiosity and without any piety, or even with dishonest intentions, do not have those feelings.

A nun writes:

> "I firmly believe in the conversions that happen in Medjugorje because I myself experienced a conversion through that meeting with Our Lady, and through Sacramental reconciliation with God. On the outside, there is nothing unusual, but it is my viewpoints that have changed. Then, I did not know that Our Lady's name is: 'Queen of Peace.' I experienced then in my heart a reconciliation with all of whom I did not have good relations. I was able to forgive all injustices done to me and ardently pray for those to whom I did something wrong or had offended. I personally consider this experience a greater miracle than if I had seen Our Lady with my own eyes."

In the church in Medjugorje, the Mass is celebrated every evening. The faithful usually participate in great number and the church is filled to capacity, especially on Saturdays, Sundays, and on special occasions. Our Lady made known her wish that this Mass always be celebrated as a remembrance of her apparitions.

THE VISIONARIES, AT THE TIME THE APPARITIONS BEGAN

Vida (Vicka) Ivankovic, born September 3, 1964, has seven other brothers and sisters. Her father is a laborer, doing temporary work in Germany. She has finished a year in a textile school, and interrupted her studies when the apparitions began. The reason is that before the beginning of the school year 1981/82, Our Lady said to the visionaries that she would like one of the older seers to remain with Jakov in the parish. Vicka then voluntarily interrupted her studies and remained home. She wanted to enter a convent.

Mirjana Dragicevic, born March 18, 1965, has one brother. Her father is an X-ray technician. The family lives in Sarajevo where Mirjana attends high school. In the school year 1982/83 she was in her fourth year. The family stems from Bijakovici, and Mirjana comes there for vacation with her relatives. According to the recommendation of Our Lady, she wishes to finish high school and college.

Maria (Marija) Pavlovic, born April 1, 1965, has two sisters and three brothers. Her father is a farmer. She attended a school for hairdressers in Mostar. Previously, she stayed with her relatives in Mostar and came home Saturdays and Sundays. In the school year 1982/83, she went to school every day from home. She decided to go to a convent. From her childhood on, she stands out among other seers because of her piety.

Ivanka (Ivica) Ivankovic, born June 21, 1966, has an older brother and a younger sister. Her mother died in April 1981. Her father is also a temporary laborer in Germany. The grandmother lives with them. They have a house in Mostar, but often visit their relatives in Bijakovici. Ivanka attended high school in Mostar.

Ivan Dragicevic, born May 25, 1965, is one of four children. In the fall of 1981 he went to the Franciscan seminary in Visoko by Sarajevo, and 1982, in the fall, he tranferred to the seminary for boys in Dubrovnik. His father is a farmer.

Jakov (Jaksa) Colo, born March 6, 1971, lives with his mother in Bijakovici. His father works somewhere near Sarajevo and rarely comes home. From his first marriage he has two daughters and from the second marriage only Jakov. Jakov attended elementary school in Medjugorje. He started going to school a year earlier than usual. He is the poorest of all visionaries.

Ivanka and Vicka are cousins, and so are Mirjana and Jakov.

OUR LADY AND THE SEERS

At every apparition, Our Lady prayed with the seers. Prayer is often the main content of the apparitions. It is known that in Lourdes, Our Lady prayed only the Glory Be with Bernadette. Here, she prays all the prayers with them except the Hail Mary. It is evident that Our Lady wants to tell us all that we should pray a lot. Many presented themselves to the seers and asked them that they be recommended to Our Lady, particularly sick people. Some recommend their dear ones—sinners, so that the Mother of God would convert them. The visionaries ask Our Lady questions, either for themselves or for others who ask them to ask Our Lady something. They also sing to Our Lady. When asked which song she likes best, Our Lady answered: *Christ, in Your Name. . .* (It is her favorite obviously because of the words and not because of the melody!)

Our Lady talks to the seers and teaches them. If they are not all together, Our Lady sometimes informs them of the others, either on her own, or when they ask. It seems that sometimes she lets them know of things and events that they could not have otherwise known on their own. The whole manner and relationship of Our Lady with the children has a special sincerity and familiarity, almost intimacy, as a good mother; the best mother, who has motherly conversations with her children and teaches them all they need to know in life. Vicka says that during the midnight apparition on September 20, 1981, she even kissed her and Jakov. She calls the children "my angels," just as mothers, especially in that region, often endearingly call their children.

Our Lady showed the seers Heaven, and at least three of them saw Hell and Purgatory. The others did not wish to see them, and so Our Lady did not show them. The seers maintain that Our Lady said at that occasion:

> *I am showing you this so that you will know what reward is awaiting the ones who live according to God's will and what punishment awaits those who do not obey Him.*

In the vision of Heaven, Ivanka recognized her mother and another deceased person. Ivanka saw her mother several times.

In the fall of 1981, during an apparition in Jakov's house, Vicka and Jakov were alone. Jakov's mother knew that they were in the other room and when she came in a little later, they were not there. She looked for them in the neighborhood, but could not find them anywhere. When she returned to the room, she found both of them there. They told her that Our Lady simply took them by the hands and took them to Heaven. So, they had disappeared for about twenty minutes. Ivan also experienced something similar in the seminary in Dubrovnik.

Once during an apparition, when the children were praying the rosary, someone made a mistake, and they all laughed. But then, somewhat frightened, they looked at Our Lady, who only smiled at them. They quickly collected themselves again, and continued to pray.

It is interesting to observe the characters of the individual visionaries. Each one of them is completely different than the others; the differences are quite considerable, and yet, all found themselves together in this great undertaking of Our Lady. It can be seen in them, that they are fully aware of their duty and mission, and that is to be messengers and carriers of Our Lady's messages to the world, and that the graces they receive belong more to all others than to themselves.

Previously, Ivan was very shy, bashful and withdrawn. He avoided the company not only of older persons, but also that of persons of his own age. The apparitions brought a great change in him. He became more courageous and sociable. He acquired a certain assurance in his behavior among people.

Ivanka was also bashful. No one for example, could persuade her to do a reading in the church for the Mass. But, a week after the beginning of the apparitions, she publicly came forward in the church, together with other seers, to give her testimony.

Before the apparitions, Ivan even used to go far out of his way around an older man from his village, only to avoid greeting him. And now, he too, came forward with the others to give his testimony. This is certainly a good and positive development of human character under the influence of the great graces that the apparitions of Our Lady bring to the seers, although their own problems, struggles and crosses still remain.

None of them became a better student than he or she was before. Ivan suddenly decided to enter the seminary, only after the apparitions started, but he still had difficulties with his studies as he did before.

On the feast of Our Lady's Birthday, September 8, 1981, Our Lady appeared to Jakov and Vicka in Jakov's house. Jakov extended his hand and said: "Dear Lady, I congratulate you on your birthday!" Our Lady took his hand, and so he shook hands with Our Lady. Vicka did not dare to do it and Jakov was embarrassed, and later asked her not to tell the others, so that they would not make fun of him.

Our Lady invited Vicka and Jakov to wait for her on the 20th of September of the same year at midnight, in Jakov's house. She asked them then not to slacken off in their prayers, and to fast for a week on bread and water. Our Lady never commands anything; she only asks or recommends.

Maria said that one day, in the summer of 1981, she went into her room and found Our Lady at the window, waiting for her. She immediately called Vicka from the neighborhood. Our Lady asked them then, whether they would like to go to a convent. She said that they do not have to do it, but she would be happy if they did go. She told them to think it over very carefully because this is a decision for life. At an apparition when all seers were together, Our Lady was talking to them about the vocation to priesthood and religious orders.

The seers tell us that they sometimes even had to laugh during the apparition. Jakov, as a real youngster with his questions or answers, brings others to laughter and, of course, a motherly smile of Our Lady. Our Lady evidently has a sense of humor, that beautiful motherly humor, since she allows all this and even participates in it. Once, in the fall 1981, Jakov asked Our Lady whether or not "Dinamo" (soccer club) will be the champion and Our Lady only smiled at that question. Isn't this a warning for the conceited generation of the 20th century?: In the end, "Dinamo" actually did become the champion!

On one occasion Our Lady reprimanded Jakov for his be-

havior in school with other boys: *You have to love them all!*
Jakov replied, "I love them, but they are so boring!" Our
Lady said, *Then you have to accept it and offer it as a sacri-
fice!* "I will, my Lady, only don't tell my mother!"

CELEBRATION ON KRIZEVAC

The cross at the top of the hill, Krizevac, above Medjugorje
and the Stations of the Cross on the path to the top, certainly
has a special place in the history of the apparitions and pilgrimages in Medjugorje. Now it is clear that God had special
plans for it at the time when the parishioners were erecting
the cross—with many efforts and sacrifices.

Since the time the cross was erected, every year, in the
month of September, on the Sunday after the feast of Our
Lady's birthday, a great celebration has been held at the cross
on Krizevac. It includes Holy Mass and with traditional participation of the people from the whole region. The celebration had also been held during the time when it was forbidden
to climb the hill. But for that one day, it was permitted as
an exception.

On the second Sunday in September of 1981, there was again
a multitude of people, more than ever before in Medjugorje.
The priests estimated that there were 30,000, some said 50,000,
or even 100,000. The children asked Our Lady how many were
there: "62,000."

Since that time, there are more people and pilgrims every
year who participate in this celebration. It takes hours for
all to come down from the hill.

THE FALL OF 1981

At the beginning of the school year, 1981, in the fall, the
seers, for the most part, went their own ways. But they continued to experience their meetings with Our Lady at the time
of their evening prayers or at some other time. Only a few
times these meetings did not occur because of school duties,

or for some other reason. Vicka quit school and stayed home with little Jakov. They experienced the apparitions regularly every evening. It happened only five times that Our Lady did not come when they were expecting her.

On Saturday and Sunday, as on feast days and during vacation, the other seers joined them. Sometimes only some of them, when they came home or to their relatives, and they then experienced the apparitions together.

Maria says that she regularly experienced apparitions in Mostar where she lived during the school year, but it happened very rarely in the apartment of her relatives there. If it was at all possible, she attended the evening Mass, and there in the church, during the Mass, after Communion, she had her meeting with Our Lady. Usually, she only prayed with her and did not talk to her.

When there are more seers present at the time of the apparition, usually all would hear the questions that the others ask, or the petitions and recommendations they give to Our Lady; but it sometimes happens that they do not hear what the others ask or what Our Lady answers. If Our Lady wishes to say something only to one of them or to some of them, the others are excluded and do not hear anything. It often happens that each one talks to Our Lady at the same time and does not know or hear what the others say or what Our Lady tells the others.

Mirjana had regular visions in Sarajevo, until Christmas 1982. Our Lady did not come on two occasions, but she told her in advance that she would not come. It never happened that Our Lady did not come when Mirjana expected her. If she was traveling, which did happen several times, there was no apparition. Only once she heard the voice of Our Lady on the train, but she did not see her. In July 1982, Mirjana spent some time in Switzerland. There, she also had visions.

During the apparitions to Mirjana, as well as to the other seers, Our Lady showed Fr. Jozo Zovko in jail, but he never said anything. The seers are convinced that he, too, sees Our

Lady, but he does not talk about it.

In the fall of 1981, Mirjana had to change schools in Sarajevo. In the new environment, a girl forced her friendship on Mirjana and called her to go out with her in the evening. Mirjana did not go. Then Our Lady told her during an apparition that she should break any connection with the girl, because she wanted to lure her into drugs.

In Sarajevo, in the small living room of Mirjana's apartment, there were sometimes other people present during the apparition. Our Lady came to her when she was free from school duties. She would kneel and pray until Our Lady came. Everyone who was present says, that Mirjana was as filled with reverence as if this were the first apparition.

It happened several times that Our Lady told Mirjana to go to Medjugorje. Whenever she had some special message, Our Lady wished that all the seers be together.

In the same way, Our Lady sent Mirjana to Medjugorje when little Jakov refused to go to school. He said that Our Lady was enough for him. Our Lady then sent Mirjana to talk him into going back to school. They are cousins. Jakov's mother and Mirjana's father are brother and sister.

Ivanka had regular meetings with Our Lady in Mostar. During vacations and often over the weekend, she would come to Bijakovici and then experience the apparition with the others.

Ivan had finished the first year of high school in the Franciscan seminary in Visoko near Sarajevo, but had to go to summer school to make up some grades. He always had difficulties with his studies. While there, he experienced regular apparitions, except for a short time, around eight days in the fall of 1981. In the fall of 1982, he transferred to the seminary in Dubrovnik, where he passed the make-up exam and continued his second year of high school. There he also had regular apparitions. They occurred in such a way that others did not take notice.

PART TWO

MOTHER OF HER PEOPLE

Five More Years Unfolded With Our Lady

OUR LADY TEACHES THE SEERS AND PEOPLE HOW TO PRAY

Medjugorje became a place of prayer in a special way. Today's Christians pray so little. Therefore, Our Lady comes again to teach us to pray. During every apparition she prays with the seers and with all who are present. She wishes to stress again the value of prayer and to teach us how to pray. She is appearing in a region where, under the Turkish yoke, through the centuries, just the basic Christian prayers—the Creed, Our Father, Hail Mary and Glory Be—were the prayers that the Christian believers knew how to pray and which they prayed every single day. And just by these prayers, the people retained their faith in spite of impossible conditions and frequent persecutions.

Therefore, these prayers have a special tradition here. Our Lady now wants to show their value and importance to the whole world. From this tradition, it developed that during every apparition the Creed, seven Our Father's, Hail Mary's and Glory Be's are prayed.

On the second day of the apparitions Mirjana's grandmother suggested to the children that they pray these prayers. They obeyed and prayed up to the seventh Our Father and then experienced the apparition. They realized then that they should pray like this every day. Our Lady later confirmed that this was her wish and also recommended they add the Creed. Our Lady recommends these prayers daily as a minimum in a Christian life, as the least that each Christian should pray every day. She wishes that these prayers are said for her intentions—and the conversion of sinners.

During their meetings with Our Lady, the seers have learned how to pray. This was, for them personally, perhaps the greatest grace they received from the apparitions. Or can we perhaps imagine that anyone else could teach us to pray better than Our Lady?! The seers pray with all the strength of their bodies and their hearts. Anyone who observes them will not be tempted to doubt that their whole heart and being is praying; that their prayer is actually a prayer of a living faith, unwavering hope and a great and ardent love.

Around Christmas in 1980, a villager from Medjugorge cried bitterly because his sons were so indolent that they did not want to go to Mass, even on Christmas. Now, those same sons are in church every Sunday and almost every evening, close to the altar, in ardent and sincere prayer.

Many people testify that Medjugorje breathes and actually radiates the presence and the closeness of God that is felt and experienced there, maybe more than any place else on earth, even Lourdes and Fatima. Many, in fact innumerable people, learned to pray here or returned to prayer which they had neglected for years. Even the confessions are more sincere here and reach to the depth of the soul and transform the whole being. Here, the Word of God is accepted more vigorously and more effectively. It encompasses and transforms a person. The assumption is to come with an open heart, contrite and ready to accept the graces which are offered so abundantly here.

OUR LADY—MOTHER OF HER PEOPLE

The statements of the visionaries about how Our Lady looks at the people that are present during the apparition are significant. It was on the hill that she even turned to look at every individual; the same happened at the apparition in the small chapel in the church, and elsewhere. She cares for every person. She is indifferent to no one.

Our Lady has often emphasized that she wishes to be with the faithful. Did her Son not say, *Where two or three are gathered in My name, I am among them.* (Mt. 18:20). Is it not said in the Book of Wisdom: *The children of man are my joy.* (Sayings 8:31). Did Jesus not relate to the apostles in that way? At the Last Supper He allowed John to put his head on His chest. According to the event at Gethsemane, when Judas kissed Jesus, it shows that it was customary for Jesus and His disciples to kiss at coming and going, as it was for Jews and elsewhere in the East. It should not surprise us that Our Lady once kissed Vicka and Jakov when they promised to fast on bread and water for a week.

On August 2, 1981 after the apparition and the celebration in the church, Our Lady appeared to the visionary Maria Pavlovic in her home and told her to tell everyone in the neighborhood to come to the threshing-floor, down below the houses. Maria was somewhat confused. Who was she to call all these tired people to come to the threshing-floor? But she obeyed.

About 40 people gathered on the threshing-floor. The seers were present except for Vicka and Jakov, and a "significant event" happened. When the seers and the people started to pray, Our Lady appeared, and through Maria, invited all present to touch her. The people came one by one to Maria, who showed them where they could touch Our Lady. Dirty fingerprints remained on Our Lady's dress from many of the touches. When Our Lady departed with the "stained" dress, Maria started to cry bitterly. One of the villagers asked her, "What is it, Maria? What happened?" She replied, "Oh what, what is it with me? Why shouldn't I cry! Don't you see how Our Lady left all soiled?" And still crying, Maria told them what happened, how the people with their touches "stained" Our Lady. The villager then loudly cried out: "Brothers! Sisters! In the morning, all to confession!"

This cry was not in vain because in the next few days quite a number of villagers came to confession. It is interesting that in this case, as in all similar cases, none of the seers remembered which person "stained" Our Lady. Our Lady keeps the secret of human consciences. (Janko Bubalo, *A Thousand Meetings with Our Lady in Medjugorje,* page 80.)

A nun (who was quoted before) was present at an apparition in 1981:

"Several of us gathered in the home of the youngest seer, Jakov. In addition to the six chosen ones, there was also a girl and several other children. At exactly 6:30, everyone knelt down, blessed themselves and started to pray the Our Father. I was so excited that I don't know how much we prayed. Vicka had three small nylon bags of objects, which she gave to Our Lady to bless. Then she took the hand of the girl who was present and touched Our Lady with her hand. Maria asked me if I would like that too. Of course I accepted. She took my right hand and raised it to Our Lady's shoulder. She told me that I had touched her, although I did not see anything or feel anything physical.... However, the inner experience that I had at the meeting with Our Lady absorbed me tremendously. Inside me, some 'hills' were toppled, some 'valleys' filled in, some crooked paths straightened...(*Lk.* 3:5)."

One young nun visited Mirjana in Sarajevo and often attended the apparitions. Several times she, too, "touched" Our Lady. On such occasions, Our Lady always extended her arms, while when others touched her, she had her hands folded. When Mirjana asked her for the reason, she answered that she would soon take with her the ones to whom she extends her arms. When the sister heard that, she cried for joy that she would soon die and see Our Lady.

That same nun once came to Mirjana at a time when Our Lady no longer appeared to her on a daily basis. She was very depressed because of extraordinary troubles that she had experienced. While she was telling Mirjana about it, a light suddenly appeared in the room and Our Lady came. She came especially for that nun to give her a message through Mirjana. After that, the sister was completely at peace.

That nun died in June, 1987, following a long illness. She suffered much but always showed extraordinary patience. She prayed to Jesus to let her complete her purgatory here on earth, and it seems that her prayers had been answered.

Another nun once asked Mirjana to ask Our Lady about her brother who was killed. Our Lady did not wait for Mirjana's question but immediately said, *I heard the question. He died in the state of grace. He needs holy Masses and prayers.* Our Lady answered questions from individuals many times about whether some deceased person was in Heaven or if they needed more prayers.

When individuals direct questions or petitions to Our Lady, it deals mostly with sick people who pray for healing. Our Lady's answers are almost always such that they do not contain any promise that the prayers will be answered as requested. Very seldom does she give a positive answer with no conditions. Sometimes she gives directions as to what is to be done. For example, to a student who had a nervous disorder, she recommended that he go to the hospital. Her answers are usually that one should daily pray the Creed and seven Our Father's, Hail Mary's and Glory Be's. Sometimes she requests the rosary in addition, and to fast on bread and water on Fridays.

It is clear that the first condition that someone's petition be answered is that he or she believes, that he or she has unwavering hope and that he or she tries to do everything that Our Lady requires in her messages. It happened sometimes that someone did as Our Lady requested and then complained that his prayers were not answered. But it did not occur to him that he did not fulfill the basic request from Our Lady, to obey and do what she asks for in her messages. Our Lady herself complained during apparitions that so few miracles occur because there is so little faith and hope. Her Son had the same complaint, as the Holy Scriptures report.

When the visionaries have many questions for Our Lady, they often become confused and do not remember to say everything. Our Lady then reminds them about it herself and gives them the answers. Mirjana gave us a report about that and Vicka also told me about it. Since February 1983, when she started to tell the seers about her life, Our Lady has not accepted any more questions and does not give any answers. There are only rare exceptions. She accepts only petitions that are directed to her, but does not give any answers.

In the summer of 1981, some of the faithful had asked the

seers to ask Our Lady to bless some objects which they brought. The seers took these objects in their hands and offered them to Our Lady to bless. Later, when the apparitions started in the chapel of the parish church, there were so many articles that it was not possible for the seers to keep them in their hands and offer them to Our Lady for a blessing. So then these objects were placed on or next to the small altar during the apparition and Our Lady blessed everything that was there. The seers tell us that Our Lady blesses the objects at the beginning of the apparition. If it happens that someone brings something to the altar later, Our Lady blesses that too. These are mostly rosaries, medals, chains, sometimes figures of Our Lady, clothing of the sick and bottles of water.

Once, when the apparitions were occurring in the homes of the seers, little Ivana, the daughter of Maria's sister was present during an apparition in Maria's home. She was about one and a half years old then. From the way the child talked about it later and repeatedly wanted to come back to that room "to see that pretty lady again," it was evident that the little girl saw Our Lady, just as the visionaries. That happened only once.

SEERS FULFILL THEIR TASK

All of the visionaries became fatigued from constant questioning and always telling the same story. Vicka receives up to fifty people a day, in addition to all the work in the house and in the field. It is therefore understandable that they sometime avoid the questioning. Every evening in the church, the pastor asks the pilgrims not to ask the children anything that is unnecessary and not to burden them. But in spite of that warning, a circle of curious people forms and the seers patiently answer to all. Little Jakov doesn't like it. In the beginning, he was somewhat glad to be the center of attention and that everyone was nice to him, but not for long. Now, immediately after the blessing, he "escapes" from the church and the crowds. He goes home or he stays with his friends.

None of the seers likes the picture-taking or the taping.

Ivanka says, "We are not movie stars!" If Jakov notices that someone wants to take his picture, he covers his face with his hands.

Everyone who has had the opportunity to get to know the seers, testifies that they are completely healthy and in every way ordinary, normal young people who do not differ from other young people their age. They are all open to the people around them, always sincere, natural and lively. But they are always serious when there is talk about Our Lady and her messages, strong and firm in their statements and opinions. Fearless! They cannot be scared by threats and persecutions. In spite of the fact that they have already been the center of attention for a long time, they remain humble, with no trace of conceit. They are, to the utmost possibility, patient with all the people who question them, but when it is necessary they are quick and witty. If humility and obedience are signs of God's work, then it can be said that they have those signs. They are not at all interested in material goods. On the contrary, they reject taking anything, as indeed do many others in Medjugorje, and give so many things completely freely.

On December 15, 1981 a priest from the outskirts of Zagreb was in Jakov's house when his mother wasn't home. He has been found there often and knows the visionaries very well. Seeing the great poverty in the house, he wanted to anonymously leave some money under the tablecloth. Jakov, as usual, was busy with something else. But he noticed this immediately, jumped up and took the money and returned it to the priest. They do not want to take anything under any circumstances, in spite of the fact that they badly need it. Only if someone offers Jakov some chewing gum or candy does he take it, but then he immediately shares it with his friends.

After the apparition is over, the visionaries attend the holy Mass as if nothing has happened. And in the evening when church ceremonies are finished, they don't return home by themselves, but mix with their friends and other young people. If someone doesn't know anything about them, he wouldn't notice any difference between them and the others. Only during prayer do they become completely different.

From the 12th to the 14th of February 1982, a group of five seminarians from Zagreb was staying in Medjugorje and they were joined by a group of three seminarians from Djakovo. One of them said to the visionaries, "I would have run away a long time ago if I were in your place." He meant that he wouldn't have been able to talk about the same thing so many times. Vicka answered him: "I would have run away too if the finger of God were not here!" The seers are aware that it is their duty to give their testimony for Our Lady and her messages, and they try to fulfill these duties as well as they can. They have to be given credit for performing their duties with such great patience. They could have become numb a long time ago from the endless repetition of the same thing. But it is evident that the special grace of God exists here to help them perform their duties.

For Christmas, 1981, the seers found themselves together again in Medjugorje. Together, they performed a special program in the Church. It was all about the apparitions; Fr. Tomislav Vlasic prepared the program with them. Fr. Vlasic had replaced the pastor, Fr. Jozo Zovko. During the program in the church, there was complete silence; everyone listened intensely and with great attention. The seers maintain that their meeting with Our Lady on Christmas day was especially beautiful.

THEY ARE NOT SAINTS—BUT THEY ARE CHOSEN

It is completely certain that the seers in Medjugorje are not saints. Perhaps someone doesn't like something that he sees about them. But that will always be something unimportant and trivial. It would not be just to expect them to be perfect in every way. They themselves were quite surprised that Our Lady came to them. It could be said that they are in no way extraordinary. But why did Our Lady select them to be the carriers of her messages? That remains a secret of God's Providence. By this selection, Our Lady probably wanted to show us that God has completely different criteria and measurements than we do. God simply takes us as we are and then continues to build on this, a work of His Grace. Our Lady does the same as her Son who, a long time ago, selected uneducated fishermen from Galilee and commanded them to conquer the world for Him.

Yet the seers certainly have a unique chance to become saints, and indeed great saints, as was the case with other visionaries, such as the visionaries in Paris (Catherine Laboure), Lourdes and Fatima. They are indeed, in a special way, participants of enormous graces and gifts from God that are given to them for their personal good. And this will, without any doubt, help them on their way toward God, to climb very high, but at the same time, make it possible to perform their mission better and more faithfully as heralds and carriers of the messages of Our Lady. But even if, later in their lives, they become unworthy of these graces and God's trust, as was the case several times with some prophets and visionaries, that does not in any way change the authenticity of the messages which God gives through them. Indeed, we must admit to the visionaries in Medjugorje, that the influence of the great graces that they receive through the apparitions is visible in them and in their lives.

IVAN'S DIARY

About the middle of September 1981, Ivan sent his diary from the seminary in Visoko to Vicka and Jakov in Bijakovici, as proof that he was having apparitions as previously.

August 28, 1981: "She did not stay long. She only told me that I was tired and exhausted and that I should rest so that I will be rested tomorrow. In addition she said: *Go in God's peace. Amen.*" (On that day Ivan arrived at the seminary.)

August 29, 1981: "Our Lady appeared to me. I asked her how things are in our village. She smiled and said: *My angels perform their penance well.* I asked her whether she was going to help us in school. She said that God's help exists everywhere. *Go in God's and Jesus' peace and with my blessing. Amen. Goodbye.*"

August 30, 1981: "I asked her again how things are in our village. She repeated the same: *My angels perform their penance in every place and at all times.* I also asked her how it is going to be for us in God's house. She said: *Do not be afraid, I am with you in each place and in every time. Go in God's peace with the blessing of Jesus and me. Amen. Goodbye.*"

August 31, 1981: "I asked her whether the people in our village are pious. She answered: *Your village is now the most pious parish in Hercegovina, and in your village there are quite a few individuals who are outstanding in piety and faith.* Then a heart and a cross appeared, shining on a picture of Jesus, and then it disappeared. (He meant the picture of Jesus in the seminary chapel.) When Our Lady was leaving she said: *Go in the peace of God, with the blessing of Jesus and me. Amen. Goodbye.*"

September 1, 1981: "I prayed with her to help me with Jesus' task and for Jesus' inspiration. Then all the seminarians prayed the rosary for a good beginning of the school year, for good health and for every progress in this life. Our Lady smiled and showed signs of a good state of mind (perhaps benevolence?). She told us not to be afraid because she is with us and firmly guards us. Then a cross and the Heart of Mary appeared and she said: *Go in God's peace. Amen. Goodbye.*"

September 2, 1981: "I asked blessings for Ante, Dario, Miljenko and myself (these are my companions in the seminary, also from the parish of Medjugorje). She said: *You are my children and my children you remain. You started on Jesus' way and no one can prevent you from spreading Jesus' faith.* She said only: *A firm faith, my angels!* At that moment she disappeared. In parting she said: *Go in God's peace, my angels, with the blessings of Jesus and me. Amen. Goodbye.*"

September 3, 1981: "I studied in the study hall. Suddenly, a light appeared and flashed exactly in front of me. We talked much and smiled in silence. Fifteen minutes passed. Then she went to the large picture of Pope John Paul II and firmly hugged him with a smile on her face. She lead the prayer and I followed. Then she disappeared after she said:
Go in God's peace, my angel. Amen. Goodbye."

September 4, 1981: "I asked her about the sign and she only smiled and said: *You children are impatient, my angels.* She left quickly saying: *Go, my angels, in God's peace. May God's blessing be with you. Amen. Goodbye.*"

September 5, 1981: "I was praying in the chapel. She came while I was praying the Our Father. She said: *Praised be Jesus.* She prayed with me the entire time. When she was leaving she said, *Go in God's peace and God's blessing be with you. Amen. Goodbye.*"

September 6, 1981: "I was praying in the chapel. Suddenly, a great light appeared. After that, she told me to pray every Sunday until she sends the great sign and God's gift. We prayed ardently and undisturbed that God may see his great children. We prayed until 7:30 and then she said: *Go in peace, my angel. May God's blessing be with you. Amen. Goodbye.*"

September 7, 1981: "I was praying in the chapel when she came, smiling, and said: *Convert, all of you who still remain. The sign will come when you convert. Amen. Goodbye.*"

September 8, 1981: *I ask only for firm prayer. It should be prayed with your life, so that true faith can be realized from the roots. This is my message for today. Go in God's peace. Amen. Goodbye.*

September 9, 1981: "When she came, the whole chapel flashed with light and a big red cross appeared on the picture of Jesus. Then she said: *Praised be Jesus.* That evening we prayed seven Our Fathers, one decade of the rosary and the Creed. When she was leaving, a cross and a heart appeared. *Go in God's peace. Amen. Goodbye.*"

September 10, 1981: "We prayed together and sang, but mostly prayed. These prayers were full of joy, full of love and heart. Then she said: *Go in God's peace, my angel. Amen. Goodbye.*"

September 11, 1981: "We only prayed and sang. She was all in gold. She was shining. Then she said: *Go in God's peace, my angel. Amen. Goodbye.*"

September 12, 1981: "I was praying in the chapel for about half an hour. Suddenly a light flashed in different colors. At that moment she appeared in prayer and said: *Praised be Jesus.*

Then she started to pray and at the moment when she was departing she said: *The sign will come in time. Go in God's peace, my angel. Amen. Goodbye."*

September 13, 1981: "All of us in the seminary were praying after confession. We prayed the entire rosary. She came to the picture of Jesus and said: *This is your Father, my angel.* And she prayed with us. She was smiling and was in a happy mood. *Go in God's peace, my angel. Amen. Goodbye."*

At every apparition, Our Lady never prays the "Hail Mary" but always prays the "Our Father" and immediately after that the "Glory Be."

FALSE RUMORS ABOUT MEDJUGORJE

Since our religious press, with rare exception, does not report about Medjugorje and the events that happen there, people talk about them and spread the news by word of mouth. It is clear that by doing so, the imaginations of some get carried away and there is talk of all kinds of things that are positively not true. That is understandable, because this always happens among people. At first, during the first years, there was more of it, but today it is not that much, because we have various books and leaflets which explain about Medjugorje and the messages of Our Lady.

In the foreign press, the information is also sometimes not exact, but today the faithful in European countries and in the whole world are quite well informed about Medjugorje, much better than we who are so close to the origin. A small library already exists containing different publications about Medjugorje. Religious and secular publications often write about it. With time their writing becomes more exact and objective.

WHY SO MANY APPARITIONS OF OUR LADY?

Since the apparitions are lasting this long and occur every day, the seer Maria commented:

"The priests are mostly confused by the frequency
of the apparitions and they ask us why Our Lady
has been coming for such a long time. All we know
is that she is coming and that we see her. In the
beginning we thought that she was coming only for
us and for our parish, but later we realized more
and more that her messages pertain to all of
mankind."

Many priests and bishops have a conception about the apparitions of Our Lady in Lourdes, Fatima and other places
and therefore have doubts about the verity of the apparitions
in Medjugorje because Our Lady has been coming for such
a long time and so often, to be exact every day. (It happened
only five times that Our Lady did not come when the children
expected her, and that was all during the first few months
of the apparitions.) This does not in any way fit the knowl-
edge that we all have about previous apparitions of Mary.
In addition, the apparitions in Medjugorje are different in many
ways from other apparitions that we know about. And the
longer they last, the greater the differences become.

The seers related all of these doubts and complaints to Our
Lady. Our Lady smiled and answered: *Are you getting bored
with me? Everything is developing exactly according to God's
plan. Be patient. Persevere in prayer and penance...Every-
thing will come at the right time...* The call for patience
is in relation to the promised sign that would give certainty
to all who want to believe, but who say that they do not have
"enough reason" to believe.

OTHER APPARITIONS OF OUR LADY
IN OUR HOMELAND

In the years after the last war, there was much talk about
various apparitions of Our Lady in our provinces. It is my
opinion that most of these alleged apparitions were a fruit
of fantasy and some of them even the devil's deceit. I am
ready to admit that at least some of them were true apparitions
of Our Lady. I would even say, a preparation for what we

are experiencing today in Medjugorje. For example, the alleged apparitions in Rozenica, a parish in Pokupsko, started exactly thirty years before the Medjugorje events. I think it is definitely necessary to give more attention to those apparitions, if there are still any witnesses or documents about them available.

But even with the events of Medjugorje, there has been talk of other apparitions of Our Lady in our homeland, in several places in Hercegovina and elsewhere. The most well-known are the apparitions in Gala by Sinj. Fr. Franc Franic, the Archbishop of Split, established a special commission for the purpose of investigating the apparitions in Gala. The Church must examine all these cases and make a judgment about them, just as about Medjugorje. I personally believe that at least some of these apparitions are true, and that we are dealing with so-called "surface apparitions," similar to the cases during the time of the apparitions in Lourdes and Fatima.

Sometime around the end of winter or the beginning of spring in 1982, on the initiative of the pastor from Izbicno, the children in Medjugorje asked Our Lady why there are so many signs in Hercegovina. Our Lady answered: *My children, did you not notice that the faith began to vanish? Many come to church only because they are accustomed to coming. It is necessary to awaken the faith—this is a gift from God.*

HOW I EXPERIENCED MEDJUGORJE

Finally, my long-time dream was fulfilled! I came to Medjugorje after I had spent four full months living solely for Medjugorje and the messages of Our Lady. I arrived on a Thursday, April 29, 1982 in the afternoon. My first and greatest wish was to be present at the apparitions of Our Lady on every single evening of my stay in Medjugorje.

I was told to come at quarter to six in the evening, to the small chapel across from the sacristy, where Our Lady regularly appears a little after six o'clock (at the time when Mass begins in the church). I found about 15 people there, among them a few nuns. About five minutes before six, Vicka and

Jakov arrived. They came very simply. Vicka greeted everyone with "Praised be Jesus" and immediately went to the
sisters she knew and kissed them and some other women she
knew.

Someone gave Vicka a piece of paper with questions and
petitions to Our Lady. I saw that she also brought a few with
her. I gave her a paper on which I had typed my petitions
and questions and a letter that the Superior of one of our
Carmelites had written for Our Lady. Vicka took everything,
read it, and placed it in front of her on the altar. She stood
close to the altar. Jakov stood next to her and hugged her
like a child who hugs his mother closely. Jakov closed the
door and after the Mass had begun in the church they stood
there, folded their hands, made the sign of the cross and started
to pray the Our Father, Hail Mary and Glory Be, and all
present prayed with them. We prayed everything together.

And so it went—the first, the second, the third and the
fourth Our Father. Then I thought that maybe Our Lady
wouldn't come because of me. Then we started the fifth: "Our
Father. . ." and stop! At that moment Vicka and Jakov fell
on their knees, perfectly synchronized, even the best drilled
group of soldiers couldn't do better. Our Lady was here. Everyone knelt. Silence. I knelt a little to the side of Vicka. I couldn't
see her face. She raised her head a little, her hands were
folded on her chest so that the fingers of one hand covered
the folded fist of the other hand. Jakov did likewise. After
a time Vicka suddenly broke the silence with, ". . .Who art
in heaven. . ." All of us then followed the praying of the Our
Father that Our Lady had started, and prayed together with
her. Without any pause, as if she always prayed that way, Vicka
prayed the Glory Be. Our Lady prayed with us and since she
cannot pray to herself, omitted the Hail Mary. After that there
was silence again. Then after a time, Vicka, in low tones ut-
tered a sigh: "She is gone." (Ode!) The two of them stood
up. Jakov immediately escaped somewhere, I did not see where
or when. (He was in the church by the altar with other children.) Vicka retreated and sat on the bench next to a nun.

Now I could see Vicka's face from time to time. In her

eyes I saw Heaven. Her face and eyes radiated an expression that I have never seen on anyone else; a miraculous sweetness, joy, happiness, bliss. Ecstasy radiated from her eyes and covered her face. On that same day, in the afternoon, I met Vicka in her home in Bijakovici, but that expression was not on her face then. I noticed it for a time during the prayers over sick people, when the Franciscans prayed behind the altar with extended arms, and the visionaries sat behind them on chairs. That expression clearly testified that those eyes—a moment before—saw Heaven on earth.

I was present at apparitions on two more evenings. The second evening Maria was with the two of them and the third evening Ivanka also joined them. The second evening I stood next to the altar at the window, so that I could better see the faces of the seers during the apparition, but I had miscalculated. The altar table was full of various articles that the faithful had brought and placed there to be blessed by Our Lady, all mostly in plastic bags, along with several bottles of water. When the visionaries again fell to their knees (again as if they'd been chopped down), because of these articles, I could not see their faces. I tried to lean a little to the right behind the person who knelt before me, to see their faces, but I didn't succeed. I attained only that I had ruined my own mood from the first evening which came over me beautifully because of the presence of Our Lady. Jakov was between Vicka on his left and Maria on his right.

The third evening I stood between the door and the altar. I was late because I heard confessions before the Mass and the chapel was almost completely full. During the apparition I could clearly see the faces of all three girls. I couldn't see Jakov's face because he was so small that he was hidden by the altar. The eyes of all three of them were wide open and they stared immovably at a point on the wall, exactly where the crucifix hangs, or a little below it. Their heads were raised a little but it did not spoil the harmony of their appearance.

The facial expressions of Maria and Ivanka did not change the whole time, at least I didn't notice it. The expression was very beautiful, bright but serious, and yet far from the expression on Vicka's face. Everything was just as it was the first evening. Her expression changed—one moment it was a smile—a special smile that is impossible to describe, so beautiful that you could watch it always. Then her face became more serious, but the basic expression remained constant. I noticed that all three moved their lips, but slowly, not as fast as when one talks normally. Everything else was the same as the first evening. At the end, Vicka again said, "She is gone."

On the third evening there were four seers. After the usual preparations and right after the beginning of the Mass, all four stood in front of the altar: Ivanka, Jakov, Vicka and Maria. They didn't even finish the first "Our Father who art in heav. . ." and all four were again on their knees as before. The apparition lasted five to six minutes the first evening (I didn't look at my watch when it started), and the other two evenings about six minutes or a little more. On the third evening Ivanka and Vicka sighed, "She is gone," but not together. I could clearly distinguish both words "gone" with a difference of a fraction of a second.

What did I feel during the apparitions? Our Lady, the Queen of Peace, Mother of my Savior and God and my Mother, is here, present in body and soul, only about two meters from me, and on the second evening only a meter from me. I didn't see anything special, except the visionaries in front of me. But within me, my heart was burning. Even with my best efforts, I cannot describe exactly what I felt, especially on the first evening. The feeling of the presence of Our Lady grasped me so that no power in the world could shake me in my belief that Our Lady was really there. I think I will never in my life forget what I had experienced in my soul in those moments.

A long time ago, I had an ardent desire to visit any place that Our Lady came to on this, our miserable earth. And for me, this long unattainable wish was now realized, because I visited Banneux and Beauraing in Belgium several times, as well as Lourdes and Fatima. In Fatima, I experienced unforgettable moments. But this is above everything else; just like Heaven over the earth. At the other places there were traces of Our Lady's footprints left so many years ago. But here, she herself is alive and truly present. And what a joy for me to celebrate Mass those three days on that same altar, and stand on the same spot where she stood the evening before! Is it unusual then, that after three days, I could not break loose from this blessed place? My heart remains there...

At a sign of peace, Vicka stood up on the first evening and extended her hand to each one of us with much warmth and cordiality. Even Jakov came from somewhere and extended his hand to everyone in his delightful, childish way. On the following evenings it was similar, but they didn't have time to shake hands with everyone. For Holy Communion, they both went to the front of the altar and received, standing next to the altar boys. Vicka returned to our chapel and knelt down in a corner to give thanks, immersed deeply in prayer to the One whose Mother she saw a moment ago with her own eyes. Jakov knelt next to her. But after a short time, while Communion was still being distributed in the church, Vicka stood up and went to see some people to tell them Our Lady's answers to questions and petitions. It seemed to me that these people had to leave early and they needed the answers quickly. She did not come to me. After the end of the prayers over the sick, which the Franciscans perform in the church, Vicka returned to the chapel and called me to the side to tell me the answer from Our Lady. She did not need to look at the papers. She knew exactly what answer to give to each person. There was no mistake. A little later she returned my paper and the letter from the Reverend Mother. But on Sunday morning, when I asked her to repeat to me Our Lady's answer to my petition, I had to remind her what it was about, because she could not remember exactly—but she knew what Our Lady had answered.

On Saturday, I asked Jakov whether he knew what answer Our Lady had given to my questions. He said he didn't know anything. He also had pieces of paper with questions and petitions for Our Lady. I didn't talk about it with anyone, but I have the impression that each seer transfers messages and questions to Our Lady at the same time and each receives answers from Our Lady, but they do not hear what the others ask or what answers they receive. I know from previous statements of the visionaries, that Our Lady talks to all of them together, that all hear and understand the things which concern all of them, but sometimes she excludes one or even all the rest of them and talks only to the one who is concerned. It seems she did so in that case too.

Immediately after the Mass, all of the visionaries kneel down behind the altar in the church with a friar on each side of them. Then a Franciscan begins to pray the Creed—the longer one—the so-called Nicean Creed which is prayed in the Mass. Then the seers lead the prayers of the seven Our Fathers, Hail Marys and Glory Be's. After that a Franciscan starts the "Hail Holy Queen." Following, two or more Franciscans, stand behind the altar and extend both arms in front of them. One of them prays a prayer for the sick (which is not always the same) and which seems to be improvised for a specific occasion. In the beginning, the visionaries prayed that prayer also, or silently followed the prayer with extended arms. But that was too strenuous for them, so they introduced the custom that the seers sit on chairs behind the altar during this prayer. The people who are seriously ill are later seated in these chairs and the seers come to each of them, place both hands on the head of each, and pray over that person for a long time.

GETTING TO KNOW THE SEERS

I arrived in Medjugorje on a Thursday, in the early afternoon. After a short visit to the church and reporting to the parish house, I went to Bijakovici, and was directed to the home of Vicka. I arrived at about three o'clock. In the kitchen was Vicka's grandmother, a deaf old woman, sitting on the couch and praying her rosary. Also present was Vicka's younger sister, who had a bandaged arm which she had broken that spring. Behind them, on the couch, Vicka was asleep. She stood up when I entered. I was embarrassed that I woke her up, but what could I do, for I didn't know that she would be asleep. There was a very cold wind that day and she had been planting tobacco and was tired from all the activities, and had a headache. But she didn't show even a trace of annoyance or impatience that I woke her. Actually, I wasn't ready for a conversation with her and only asked her what came to my mind. I just wanted to arrange for a later meeting, thinking that I had enough time, but I was mistaken. On Friday she was planting tobacco all day. On Saturday she was with Jakov in Split and I could catch her for only ten minutes before the first Mass on Sunday morning. But here, too, I was unlucky because two acquaintances from the outskirts of Varazdin delayed her in front of the church, and she was late getting to me. She would have to break into pieces to satisfy everyone!

I wasn't with Vicka long when a young boy suddenly appeared and Vicka introduced him: "This is Jakov." The first thing I said to him was, "Well, Jakov, 'Dinamo' is the champion! What do you say to that?" He only laughed happily. He took the chewing gum and candy that I offered him and immediately shared them with Vicka and her sister.

Outside, on an asphalt-covered village road, a group of boys his age or a little older, were playing ball. "Boys, who are you for, Dinamo or Velez?" (The day before, Velez beat Dinamo in Mostar.) Five or six voices resounded in unison: "For Dinamo and Cibona!" Jakov probably played ball with them, because he loves to play ball.

Maria came home on Friday afternoon. I only saw her in the evening during the apparition and later arranged to meet her at her house on Saturday afternoon. However, she was also planting tobacco and helping her mother, so that I found her only on the second try. She had just returned from the tobacco field and excused herself that she was dirty because she didn't have a chance to change. She is tall and slim like Vicka, but completely different from Vicka. Vicka is tempermental and lively and Maria is very quiet, calm and shy. A married couple that I know, were there to see her too. They wanted to see and hear her. She is already used to such curiosity. But when they wanted to tape our conversation, she was so opposed to it, that I had to tell them not to do so. She answered the questions nicely and quietly. She confirmed that she regularly experiences apparitions in Mostar too. She would like to go to a convent. "To Bijelo Polje?" "I don't know yet."

I wanted to visit Jakov's home too. I asked him whether his mother was home. No, she was in the field. She works for others. I saw that he didn't want to take me to his house, which is below the village, so I didn't insist.

Ivanka came to Bijakovici on Saturday, late in the afternoon, so I couldn't meet her personally or talk to her. On Saturday, Ivanka was praying over the sick people for a long time and I couldn't wait for her. I "caught" Vicka and arranged to meet her on Sunday morning. I asked her to invite Ivanka too, but she said this would probably not be possible. I hoped that Mirjana would come from Sarajevo, but she didn't.

THE FIRST ANNIVERSARY

It was in the beginning of April, 1982, that Mirjana, one of the seers, asked Our Lady during an apparition, whether she would like her own special feast day. Our Lady answered that she wished that June 25th, the day she first talked to the children during the apparition, be celebrated as the feast day of the "Queen of Peace." It will take a long time for the Church to officially establish such a feast day, but the faithful people understood the wish of Our Lady and accepted it whole-heartedly, especially because that year was the first anniversary of the apparitions of Our Lady in the parish of Medjugorje.

On Thursday, June 24, 1982 on the Feast Day of St. John the Baptist and the first anniversary of the first apparition, many people came to Medjugorje. There were several thousand people. Many came from distant places by bus. After the usual evening ceremonies in the church it was arranged ahead of time that there would be a vigil in the church. people sang to Our Lady and prayed until midnight. After that, the church remained open the entire night. All the benches were full of people. Some tried to sleep on the benches, as much as it was possible, others dozed off, then prayed again, everyone silently to himself. On the outside of the church there were even more people. There were so many that they couldn't find room in the church. People tried to sleep on the ground, under the open sky, as best they could. There was no room in the village for shelter. The hotel in Citluk could take only a small number of pilgrims. Some slept in hotels in Mostar. Most of these people went home the next morning, but others came in their place.

On Friday, June 25, there were several Masses in the morning. The church was full or almost full all the time and a big crowd was also outside the church. The climax was in the evening. In the afternoon, streams of people rushed toward Medjugorje from all sides. Many came in cars and buses, but most of them came on foot, even barefooted, from distances of up to 100 kilometers. One witness says how he watched barefooted pilgrims on the hot asphalt. They walked as if on needles; not used to walking barefooted. They raised their feet quickly and the hot asphalt literally burned them. But they continued walking persistently to their goal, where Our Lady awaited them. There were pilgrims from Macedonia, Serbia, Vojvodina, from all Croation regions, from Slovenia and from foreign countries—our people and foreigners. They all found themselves gathered around the same mutual heavenly Mother.

On that day, the temperature in Medjugorje was 95 °F in the shade. There had been no rain for a long time. They said that since Christmas, it had rained only once. There is a little shade, but it doesn't help much. The scorching heat is unbearable. During the night it gets cooler, but it is still warm. The grass is all burned out from the drought and heat. The tobacco, which at that time of year should be very high, remained small and low. It cannot grow without moisture. The vineyards looked good, but there was the danger that the drought would ruin them. This time, coming to Medjugorje certainly wasn't a pleasure for anyone, but rather a real penance for all. Our Lady in Medjugorje requests penance, and the people accepted her request and obeyed. There was ample rain a few days after the anniversary.

That evening the church was full to capacity and it was stuffy and hot as an oven. Around the church there was a multitude of people everywhere, and farther away from the church, all the roads were crowded with people. The Franciscans in Medjugorje estimate that there were 50,000 people, the greatest number ever to come to Medjugorje. They say that there were approximately as many people as in September of last year on the hill Krizevac. Others maintain that there were 100,000, which is somewhat exaggerated, but 50,000 is certainly too conservative.

Confessions were heard around the church as has now become customary. Confessions in the church were not possible because of the heat and the crowd of people. The confessors sit on regular chairs and the penitents kneel on the ground, without any support or convenience, mostly exposed to the sun. But that didn't bother anyone. They came to pray for blessings and help from Our Lady, and they know well that the first condition is to rid themselves of sin with a sincere confession. During the Mass, Holy Communion was distributed inside and outside. Another Mass was held in the chapel so that more hosts could be consecrated and it would be possible for those to receive Communion who could not receive during the Mass. On that day, 100 priests heard confessions.

On the first and second day, after the Masses, a Consecration to the Immaculate Heart of Mary was held, in accordance with the wish of Pope John Paul II and the recommendation of the Bishops' Conference. It was certainly the greatest number of faithful who ever performed such a consecration on the recommendation of our bishops.

What brought this multitude here? There is nothing here that is usually found at other pilgrimage sites, and which, unfortunately, have nothing to do with faith and piety, but rather disturb people and pull them away from their purpose for coming on pilgrimage. Here, they do not have anything to drink except the water from the cistern next to the parish house on which there is a sign: "Save the water—for drinking only!" And in this heat it is necessary to drink something. From a nun in the yard next to the parish house, you can only buy a prayer book, a rosary, or a publication of *Sveta Bastina* ("Holy Heritage"), *Glas Koncila* ("The Voice of Council"), or a pious booklet—and that is all.

These people seek something else. They firmly believe that our heavenly Mother descended here to our earth and that she still comes every day, every evening. The faithful feel and experience this closeness of Heaven on earth and come to their Mother, who is here in such an unusual way, and so close. They tell her all their wishes, prayers and needs, they open and reveal to her their hearts and souls, they find in her motherly heart, love, understanding and help for their troubles in their souls and bodies. The people realize that the Mother of God comes here because of them, because of all of us. They understand her motherly care for us, for our future and eternity. And they obey their Mother, accept her message, and put it into practice.

Many educated and wise people have hundreds of objections and thousands of difficulties in accepting Our Lady's coming here. But simple people simply accept her and obey, even when she requests conversion, a transformation of life, persevering prayer, penance and reconciliation. Here, Jesus' works come true again: *Blessed are the poor in spirit. . . (Mt. 5:3)* and *I glorify you, Father. . .for hiding these things from the learned and the clever and revealing them to children. (Mt. 11:25).*

And from full lungs and opened mouths resound the song to Our Lady of Medjugorje: "We came to you, dear Mother, from all parts of the world. We bring to you our troubles and with them our desires. Look at us, console us, place your hands on us. Recommend us to your Son. Mother of Peace, pray for us!"

People know that she has never abandoned anyone who

sought refuge from her. And therefore, they come with such faith and trust, and in such great numbers, to the throne of graces, to the Queen of Heaven and earth, to their Mother who comes here as the Queen of Peace.

During the apparition on that day, before the evening Mass, Our Lady asked the priest, through the children, to thank the people for their prayers, penance and sacrifices and asked them to be patient in expecting fulfillment of her promises. She also said that everything is developing according to God's plan. She gave a similar message somewhat earlier. The priest revealed it to all who were present. During the apparition on that day, all six visionaries were present.

THE LAST APPARITIONS OF OUR LADY?

In November of 1982, someone asked Mirjana why Our Lady has come here so often and for such a long time, and is so intimately close and completely different from other previous apparitions. Without hesitation Mirjana answered: "Because these are her last apparitions." Mirjana also said that Our Lady told them that when these apparitions come to an end, there will be false apparitions in the world and we must be very careful not to be deceived.

Opinions have been expressed from many sides, even from priests and Franciscans in Medjugorje, that it cannot be true that the apparitions in Medjugorje could be the last apparitions of Our Lady in the world. On May 2, 1982, Vicka was asked what she knew about this and she answered: "During the apparition, Our Lady literally said this: *I have come to convert people for the last time. I will not come to earth anymore.*" In order to remove any doubts, on June 25, 1982, the anniversary of the apparitions, Fr. Tomislav Vlasic asked Ivan to ask Our Lady two questions: Is this apparition of Our Lady in Medjugorje the last one? Our Lady didn't answer. And then the second question: Are these apparitions the last ones in the present world? Our Lady answered: *These are the last apparitions.* I think that Our Lady removed all doubt with her answer. Not only the apparitions in Medjugorje by themselves, but all other apparitions of the Mother of God which appear at this time in the world, are the last appearances of the Mother of God in this world.

If we closely observe the way in which Our Lady in Medjugorje appears, especially her intimate closeness with the visionaries, and with other people through the visionaries, in addition to the duration and frequency of the apparitions, we must realize from these facts that this is the utmost effort of Our Lady's love toward sinful mankind to induce it to conversion. I cannot imagine how she could humble herself more and come still closer to us. She is coming exactly in this way, as if she wants to show us all her motherly love and tenderness, in order to make it easier for us to receive and accept her messages.

Therefore, it is my opinion that all the apparitions of Our Lady that appear today in the world, together with the apparitions in Medjugorje, are indeed the last ones, and after that, Our Lady will not appear anymore, any place else.

Evidently, Our Lady wants to destroy all the conceptions that we have acquired in respect to previous experiences of her apparitions. It is as if she wants to show us that everything up to now, including Fatima and Lourdes, was only preparation for what is coming now. If we exclude the time of Christ's life on this earth, it has never happened (even the greatest and most miraculous of God's intervention in the Old Testament), that Heaven has come so far down to earth and has been so close to all of us.

We live in apocalyptic times. The power of terrible threats hangs over all of mankind. Only a blind man, or someone who makes himself blind, is not able to see this. It can easily happen that in the near future, all of mankind will be destroyed. Even without war, the destruction of the environment and the world around us already has catastrophic dimensions. And those who are responsible to human society are still blind, or do not want to see it. It may already be too late.

Now, perhaps more than at any time in history, mankind has sunk deep into unbelief. It isn't only that religion has disappeared from public life, but unbelief has also crept into Christ's Church, and entire nations have abandoned their faith almost completely in a short period of time. What is left can hardly be called Christianity. Thousands of priests and religious men and women have deserted their sacred vows and promises and left their vocation. Moreover, many of those who have not done it publicly, live a life which is not proper for their vocation and status.

If this continues, would Hell conquer the Church of Christ? According to the words of Christ, this can never happen. When all other means fail, God sends us His Mother, the Queen of Heaven, angels, the whole world and of all people; our Mother, and the Mother of the Church, in order that she would move all of God's powers in Heaven and on earth, conquer Satan and take away from him everything that he has succeeded in acquiring, and so protect us from all of the evil that is threatening us due to sin and apostasy. Our Lady came to prepare us to re-establish on earth, the Kingdom of the Holy Spirit in which her Immaculate Heart will triumph, as she announced in Fatima.

We have no other choice. Either we obey, convert and line up as those who are loyal to her, and try to spread the messages of Our Lady and convert the world, (above all with prayer and penance), or we cross over to the other side and experience the fate of the enemies of God and Our Lady. We know how it is going to be in eternity and we also know what is going to happen on earth. Our Lady clearly said, at Fatima, that some nations will completely disappear from the face of the earth if mankind does not convert. What right do we have to maintain that we are going to be an exception, if we do not obey the invitation of Our Lady?

Our world lives in the days of the greatest graces in all of history and Our Lady is offering us this at Medjugorje. Are we going to take advantage of it, or are we going to persist in unbelief and indolence until it is too late?

Dear Lady, Queen of Peace, obtain for us such powerful graces from God that we will not be able to resist them, but that we obey you, fulfill and continue to fulfill your messages, so that through us many others will be able to acquire the grace of salvation.

REVELATION AND APPARITIONS

God's revelation, which the Church transmits and which we accept with faith, tells about the living God who is more to us than a good Father who is interested in His children. This revelation of God was often given through visions and apparitions. Direct contact from God with mankind in the Old Testament, after banishment from Paradise, was in this manner. It is similar in the New Testament. God talked to people through Jesus Christ in the human form of God-Man. But His birth was announced by an apparition and after the Resurrection He appeared to His disciples, and even after His Ascension into Heaven, at Paul's conversion.

Therefore, the Church accepts, in principle, the possibility of apparitions which stimulate the faithful to do all that God, throughout history, has told us to do. In her history of almost two thousand years, the Church acknowledged such revelations as works of God and recommended them to the faithful. To differentiate between the official revelation of God, which is binding for all believers and which ended with the death of the last apostle, theologians call these revelations "private revelations." Many great movements in the Church, many devotions and even some holy days, such as the Solemnity of Corpus Christi and the holy day of the Sacred Heart of Jesus, came into being on the incentive of private revelations.

The Church always has the right and the duty to examine such private revelations and to form her judgment about them, which she then proposes to the faithful. Such is the case with Medjugorje. When the time comes, the Church will certainly express her judgment about it, to which we subject ourselves and accept in advance. But until the Church does this, we try, according to Christ's criteria (*You will know them by their fruits*, Mt. 7:16), to form our judgment and profit from the graces which God so generously gives us here.

The essential theme of the Bible is conversion to the Living God, penance and prayer. Jesus sent His apostles to continue to preach conversion to all nations. The Church continues this work of Christ. It is the goal of each priest, and every true priest undertakes everything he can to achieve it. The children, the visionaries in Medjugorje, completely fit into this mission. They call for conversion, reconciliation, penance and prayer.

Of course there are difficulties. But they existed, more or less, with all of the prophets in the Old Testament. Difficulties existed even in relation to the person of and the preaching of Jesus Christ. There, too, everything was not immediately smooth and clear. Indeed, difficulties existed always, or almost always, in private revelations too, throughout the history of the Church. That should not surprise us today. We have to be patient and trust that God will, in time, explain everything, at least as much as is necessary for us.

There are already enough signs which should be a testimony to the verity of the apparitions of Our Lady at Medjugorje for those who do not believe. Many people saw these signs and, through them, many have converted and started to believe. Our Lady announced a great sign that is to come, but for which we must wait patiently. And the secrets she tells the visionaries, again, are nothing new in the history of apparitions of Our Lady in recent time.

There is a difference from other apparitions of Our Lady in recent times in that, the children in Medjugorje do not memorize and transfer word for word all of the messages, but they transferred them in their own words.

The children relate and repeat the messages according to their particular temperament. For some this represents an obstacle to believing, while for others it is the greatest proof of authenticity because God respects freedom. After spending two days in Medjugorje, Zivko Kustic, the main editor of the weekly *Glas Koncila* ("The Voice of the Council"), wrote in his report that he sent to the Bishop of Mostar:

"It seems to me that it is not unusual if the children do not tell exactly the same thing about the same apparition, or if the same seer does not use the same words in consecutive description of the same event. Such discrepancies always happen when several witnesses report about the same event or if one person reports several times about the same thing. By the way, that is how considerably different Gospels were created about the same event of Salvation; even the words of Christ are quoted differently in different Gospels; even some data about time does not coincide..."

The children do not possess a theologian's vocabulary which would satisfy those who are familiar with theology. Therefore, the children often cannot find the proper expressions for Our Lady's answers. Often, they didn't pay attention to the expressions which were transferred through Our Lady, which created confusion for people who sent their petitions to Our Lady through the children. For example, the children would give an answer to a sick person: "Our Lady says that you will get well," when the actual answer from Our Lady was: "If he firmly believes, prays and fasts, he will get well."

Everyone is not equally ready to accept God's message and revelation. On the contrary, some are even completely closed to it and stubbornly reject the message, even when they should accept it because of the many evident proofs, especially if the message requests their conversion. Some prophets were mistreated and stoned and even the Son of God was crucified. Such a stand is not proof against the truthfulness of the revelation, but is proof that this is a work of God, because obviously, such a stand comes from sinful human nature and is often under the direct influence of Satan. Satan fights against everything that gets in his way against the work of God. If these apparitions were the result of a sick imagination, or someone's deceit, or the deceit of Satan himself, he certainly wouldn't fight against them.

All those who reject or refuse to acknowledge the coming of Our Lady to Medjugorje or who unthinkingly make statements which have no basis, should think more deeply. I am convinced that everyone who, quietly and without prejudices, thinks about the messages of Our Lady in Medjugorje, will quickly and without any special proof, realize that here, the Spirit of God is at work, and if the person has only a little goodwill, he or she will accept them with all their heart.

THE FALL OF 1982

On August 5, 1982, upon the request of the Franciscans, Vicka asked Our Lady why she doesn't talk about sacramental devotion. Our Lady answered that she has said enough about it on other occasions (in Fatima) and that this belongs with regular Church practice. When Ivan asked her whether it was necessary to again revive the message of Fatima about monthly Confession, Our Lady answered that:

> *Monthly Confession would heal many Christians and the .Church in many regions would recover by such practice.*

She added that she will give some special messages for today's mankind, *but be patient, it is not yet time for that.*

Ivan did not return to the Franciscan seminary in Visoko where he completed his first year of high school, but went to the seminary for boys in Dubrovnik, which is lead by Jesuits. But he remained registered as a Franciscan seminarian. In Dubrovnik, he passed the make-up exam in the German language and continued his studies as a second year student. There he also had regular apparitions of Our Lady.

On the Feast Day of the Assumption in 1982, Our Lady revealed the eighth secret to three seers. They said later that this secret is very grave. On November 19, the first day of the novena before the feast of the Immaculate Conception, some seers received the ninth secret from Our Lady. That secret they said was extremely grave, and the seers cried because of it.

In the spring of 1982, Vicka was ill and the same illness returned in the fall of that year. Because of that, at the end of November she went to a hospital in Zagreb for some tests. Several days later she made a statement that the physicians didn't find anything during the tests and that she feels well. There was talk (Vicka later confirmed it), that the other visionaries wanted to ask Our Lady to heal Vicka, but Vicka did not allow it.

The Franciscans in Medjugorje relate that in the spring, when Vicka was sick, Jakov, who is especially attached to Vicka, cried when he was alone in his house, because of Vicka's illness. Suddenly, Our Lady appeared to him and consoled him in her special way. She let him know that suffering is necessary because so many people, especially in big cities here and in the whole world, live as if there were no God. They live in sin and do not care about the salvation of their soul.

Sometime in the beginning of November, 1982, the guards were removed from the hill Crnica and at the place of the apparitions. But access to both hills was still forbidden.

For Christmas, 1982, five of the visionaries in Medjugorje, (all except Mirjana), saw Our Lady with the Child in her arms and she said to them, *Rejoice!* Except for the first day of the apparitions on June 24, 1981, when the visionaries saw Our Lady from a distance on the hill, that was the only time they saw her with the Child in her arms.

On New Year's Eve, Ivan asked Our Lady during the apparition, what message she had for them. What must the people do? Our Lady answered, *More praying and fasting!* After that, Ivanka was in a village house waiting for the New Year with a small group of people. At midnight Our Lady appeared to her and again said that she should persist in praying and fasting, and she wished them all a Happy New Year.

Also on New Year's Eve, Fr. Tomislav Vlasic announced that the evening holy Mass, on that evening, and every evening from now on, would be celebrated in Medjugorje for peace in the world. Therefore, in the future, this Mass would not be available for private intentions.

In the summer and fall of 1982, about ten experts and physicians came to Medjugorje. They came at different times, stayed a week or longer, and observed the events, especially the seers, and they questioned the seers. They all concluded the same thing, independently from each other. The events that occur here are completely above any human comprehension and cannot be explained in any human manner.

Among them was Dr. Ludvik Stopar, Neuropsychiatrist from Maribor, a member of the commission of experts for the examination of miracles in Lourdes. He hypnotized two of the seers, Maria and Jakov, trying to prove whether the children were telling the truth. He concluded that they are telling the truth. He studied, in detail, three cases of miraculous healing and stated that every commission would proclaim that all three healings are medically unexplainable.

On New Year's Day in 1983, in the church in Medjugorje, a new statue of Our Lady was erected, which shows Our Lady with extended arms, approximately as the visionaries describe her. Before that, there was a statue of Our Lady of Lourdes. On March 25, 1985, the Bishop of Mostar ordered the new statue be removed and replaced with the old statue of Our Lady of Lourdes as it was before. This was done.

MIRJANA SPEAKS

In an interview, Mirjana described her experiences in the meetings with Our Lady. At the beginning, the power and magnitude of the visible presence of Our Lady overwhelmed them so much that under the influence of that great impression, they fainted during the apparition. That happened several times. Later, Our Lady gave them all a special grace and strength so that they could experience their daily meetings with her without any difficulties.

Mirjana says that Our Lady told them especially that she was an ordinary woman who had lived through and experienced human misery and problems. Thus, they should come to her always, simply, with their problems, difficulties and needs just as to their mother. She is their true Mother, more than the one who gave birth to them. She knows and understands them all.

During the apparitions Our Lady often said to Mirjana that the "time of the devil" has begun, that is, the time in which the devil was allowed to work with all his power. The whole of mankind is put to the test of faith; no one is spared. It is necessary to recognize the devil in the very beginning and readily reject him with prayer, sacrifice and penance. The "devil's time" will last until the event of the first secret. Then his end will come. He will have great success. He will seduce many. When the secrets begin to occur, Satan will have nothing more to do. The people will be left to themselves.

On April 14, 1982, Mirjana had a special vision. She writes about it herself:

"On that day, as on all the other days, I knelt down and was just about to make the sign of the cross when Satan appeared. Instead of our dear Mother and her mild and sweet face, I saw a complete contrast. I always thought that people exaggerated when they tried to frighten children, describing the devil in the worst light. Now I realize that they didn't even nearly describe his monstrosity. He had black piercing eyes, full of malice and jeer, grimaced lips, horns. . . really horrible! I felt as if I were sinking. Everything was black in front of my eyes. As from a distance, or as an echo, I heard him offering me beauty, success. . . if I denounce Our Lady and God. I don't know whether I really screamed or if this came from my soul. . .'no, no, no!' Then Satan disappeared and Our Lady appeared. Immediately I felt like nothing had happened. She gave me strength. She said to me that this is the *devil's time* and this had to happen. She gave me recognition for my faith. . ."

Two secrets will occur before the great sign that Our Lady promised to give us on the hill, the place of the apparitions. The secrets will happen one after the other in short intervals of time. All the seers except Maria know the date when this will happen. Before the great sign on the hill of apparitions, in many places in the world, there will be advanced signs that will warn the world. Our Lady also said that many will start believing when the promised sign appears.

FOR MIRJANA, THE APPARITIONS CEASE

In 1982 Mirjana spent Christmas at home in Sarajevo, where she had regular apparitions until that time. A sister who was present at the apparition on Christmas Eve, tells the following:

"Only a few people were present. After the apparition, Mirjana was sad and sat down without a word. For a time everyone was silent, but then her mother asked her what was wrong. Mirjana started to cry and left the room without a word. Later, she recovered, returned to the room and said, 'This was my next to last apparition.' Our Lady would come again only tomorrow, on Christmas, only as a joy, without any revelations. She told Mirjana the tenth secret, which is particularly grave, and with it everything will end. Our Lady promised that she would come to Mirjana every year, on her birthday, March 18th, as long as she lived. The next day, Christmas, Our Lady came and stayed with Mirjana for 45 minutes."

Mirjana herself, describes her last meeting with Our Lady:

"Our Lady prepared me for this meeting for a whole month. She explained everything to me in a motherly way. She said that she accomplished the task for which she needed me. She told me that I am sufficiently informed and that I must realize that I have to return to normal everyday life, as all girls of my age. I must continue living without her motherly advice and the conversations with her which have been so necessary for my soul. She promised to always be beside me and to help me in my most difficult situations. As long as I live with God, she will help me . . .

"This last meeting with Our Lady was very hard for me. It is not possible to describe in words the pain I felt in my soul because I would not have any more regular visions. It is similar to the feeling of realizing that you have suddenly received the most beautiful thing in your life, and you are now losing it. Our Lady was aware of my torment and pain and to cheer me up she prayed with me. She asked me to sing and glorify God. I prayed the prayer that I always prayed when I was alone with her, the 'Hail Holy Queen.'

"I always remember the words of Our Lady: 'Mirjana, I selected you and told you all that is necessary. I transferred to you many horrors that you must carry worthily. Think of me and think about how many tears I shed because of them. You must always be courageous. You quickly understood my messages, and now you have to understand that I must go. Have courage. . .' The rest that Our Lady told me was for me, personally.

"The first month was really very hard for me. Our Lady called my attention to the fact that it was going to be hard. I used to fall into deep states of depression (dejection). I avoided everyone and closed myself in my room where I used to always wait for Our Lady. I cried and called to her. I felt her help and waited for my birthday. . ."

We can easily understand why Mirjana stated: "This is my most sorrowful Christmas." All who know Mirjana say that since the apparitions stopped for her, she has now become much more mature in her character and her whole inner life. Here, too, Our Lady showed herself as the best educator.

OUR LADY GIVES AN ACCOUNT OF HER LIFE

Since January 14, 1983, every evening four of the seers in Medjugorje experience something special. Our Lady tells them about her life. They will be allowed to make it public later, but they don't know when. Everyone takes notes about what he or she hears from Our Lady. This is the reason that the apparitions now last somewhat longer, about ten minutes or more. Previously, they usually lasted two to three minutes. Since that date, Our Lady does not accept any more questions and does not give any answers.

Ivan, in Dubrovnik, also receives the biography of Our Lady. For Jakov, Our Lady finished the story of her life in a short time, but she talks more and longer to the others. When questioned how this happens at common apparitions, Vicka answered: "Our Lady continues to talk to others about her life and shows them many things in pictures, and at the same time, she talks to Jakov about other things. He no longer participates in her biography."

The seers were asked whether Our Lady, in talking about her life, also mentions what she does from Heaven for the Church of God on earth, especially through her apparitions. Ivanka says that she is not allowed to say anything about it. Vicka and Maria did not answer clearly, but it seems that it can be concluded from their answers that Our Lady talks about it. Both of them stated that the biography is beautiful, and Maria's answers, particularly, are full of enthusiasm.

JELENA VASILJ AND MARIJANA VASILJ

At the end of 1982, Jelena Vasilj was an excellent pupil in the fifth grade of the elementary school in Medjugorje. One of five children, she was born and lives in the village of Medjugorje, under the hill Krizevac. (Later, a sixth child was born.) On December 15, 1982, during school hours, she heard for the first time, inside her, a voice that evidently could not have been any voice from the outside. She was confused by that voice, especially when it continued to talk to her later. She confided to her father, who first tried to calm her down, then asked advice from Fr. Tomislav Vlasic.

Fr. Vlasic visited Jelena in her family's home and talked to her and prayed the exorcism prayers over her to eliminate any eventual influence of the evil spirit, but Jelena did not show the slightest sign which would give basis for such a conclusion. On December 23, 1982, after eight days, for the first time, she saw an angel, who told her only that he comes from God. He instructed her about things in her personal spiritual life. On December 29, 1982 Jelena saw Our Lady for the first time and from then on, at least in the beginning, she saw her every day. From time to time, Jesus also appears next to Our Lady. Our Lady and Jesus talk to her primarily about things that concern her personal spiritual life.

But in the beginning, Jelena was not aware of the fact that she experienced the apparitions with her eyes closed. Later, Our Lady explained to her that the visionaries from Bijakovici see her with their eyes, listen to the voice of Our Lady with their ears, and they can even touch her. But all of this was not given to Jelena. Jelena looks at Our Lady inside herself, and in the same way, hears Our Lady's voice or the voice of the angel, often without any vision. To see Our Lady in this way, she must deeply concentrate and in such concentration, she must often pray for a long time before she can see Our Lady. Once she experienced Our Lady coming to her but she could not see her clearly. The obstacle was her frame of mind, lack of concentration. Only after she completely concentrated and was deep in prayer could she see Our Lady clearly.

In January 1983, Our Lady didn't come for 15 days, again through Jelena's own fault because she began to think that she was better than other people because she was seeing Our Lady. Only after she had looked at herself humbly and corrected what she did wrong, did Our Lady come to her again. Our Lady then told her that she had to confess her mistake.

According to Jelena's description, when Our Lady appears to her, she looks different from the way she looks to the visionaries from Bijakovici. She wears a different dress and her hair and eyes are a different color. Our Lady explained to her that she appears in different forms, but she is always and everywhere the same.

Since the Feast Day of St. Joseph on March 19, 1983, there is another visionary in addition to Jelena Vasilj. She is Marijana Vasilj, who together with Jelena, represents a new group. Marijana Vasilj is Jelena's neighbor, is in the same class in school, and they are the same age. Jelena was born on May 14, 1972 and Marijana on October 5, the same year. In spite of the same family name, they are not related.

Marijana experiences the apparitions in the same way as Jelena, that is, through inner seeing. In the beginning, and for quite a long time, she only saw Our Lady but could not talk to her and did not hear what Our Lady said. Only on

October 5, 1983 did she also receive the grace and gift of hearing Our Lady and speaking with her like Jelena. They experience the apparitions mostly during prayers in the afternoon at Jelena's house. They agree on the hour of prayer in advance.

On April 14, 1983, Our Lady dictated to Jelena the consecration prayer "To the Mother of Goodness, Love and Mercy." In this prayer many are bothered by the words, "And I pray to you for the grace that I can be merciful to you." Fr. Vlasic talked about this with Jelena. She has a simple reply:

"Our Lady apologized to me many times. She begged my forgiveness because she cannot fulfill some of my wishes, because God wants it otherwise. Thus, not only sinners ask for forgiveness, but also someone who loves you and cares for you."

On another occasion in conversation with a priest, Jelena said something like this: to be merciful toward God or Our Lady means to forgive God and Our Lady for sending us crosses and troubles and not fulfilling our prayers the way we would like them to. Therefore, we all have reasons to be merciful toward God and Our Lady. And it seems to me that too many times we are not.

On March 1, 1983, through Jelena Vasilj, Our Lady invited all parishioners to read a passage from the Gospel (*Mt.* 6:24-34) every Thursday; to read it and live it again and again. This passage deals with the care of our bodily and material needs and asks for complete trust in God's Providence: *You cannot serve God and wealth...do not be worried about your life...look at the birds...seek first the Kingdom of God and His justice...*

A NEW CALL FOR CONVERSION

Through Jelena Vasilj, Our Lady sends specially expressed messages in which she calls us to conversion. Jelena says (April 26, 1983) that during the last few days the Mother of God was sad because there are so many great sinners. She calls for conversion. Our Lady asks that we hurry with conversion.

She stresses that she needs many prayers and penance from us. Our Lady says,

> *The only word I wish to tell the world is conversion. I am saying this so that you will tell everyone. I ask only for conversion. It is not hard for me to suffer. I will suffer for you. And I beg from you only to convert. I will ask my Son not to punish you. Only convert. You do not know anything about God's plans, neither will you learn, nor can you learn what God will send you, nor what He will do. I only beg you to convert. This is my wish. Be converted. Be ready for anything, but only convert. That is all I wish to tell you. Deny yourself everything; this is part of conversion. Goodbye and remain in peace.*

Through Jelena, Our Lady repeatedly requests fasting for different occasions, in addition to the fast on Friday. But Our Lady stresses that it is not enough to fast, we must at the same time start breaking sinful and disorderly habits. She stresses that fasting doesn't have any value if we quarrel at the same time or sin in another way. Regarding disorderly conduct she specially mentions watching television, smoking, excessive partaking of strong drink. Our Lady requests from the faithful, including the children, that half an hour before holy Mass they concentrate more and get ready for it because, *Holy Mass is the greatest prayer.*

When I think about the apparitions of Our Lady in Medjugorje, the words of the prophet Joel that St. Peter quotes in his first sermon immediately after the coming of the Holy Spirit, involuntarily come to my mind:

In the last days, says the Lord, I will pour out my spirit on every human being. Your sons and daughters shall prophesy, your young men shall see visions, your old men shall dream dreams. Even on my servants, men and women, in those days, I will pour out my Spirit and they shall prophesy. I will display miracles in heaven above and signs on the earth below. The sun will be turned into darkness and the moon into blood before the great day of the Lord dawns. All who then call on the name of the Lord will be saved. (Ac. 2:17-21).

And in this last time, the words of the prophet must be fulfilled. I am convinced that they are truly fulfilled here and that this is only an introduction to greater happenings that await us in the near, actually immediate future.

APPEAL OF PRIESTS FROM MEDJUGORJE

On April 9, 1983, on the occasion of the Year of Redemption, the priests from Medjugorje directed to the priests and to the Bishop of Mostar, their special message. In it they stress: "We recognize one and the same Spirit who inspired the Holy Father and who moves our parish and larger circles of believers for 21 months already. The Church that gathers here already lives through the values that the Holy Father stresses as the primary plan."

Then they mention in detail how this is done in Medjugorje.

"On Fridays, everyone fasts on bread and water; during Lent they fast several days a week. Many fast all during Lent. Many give up alcohol, cigarettes, entertaining programs and other pleasures. The pilgrims fast a day before they leave. People experience a fundamental renewal. The confessions of the faithful are often deeply moving. The parish celebrates a common monthly reconciliation, which includes confession and days of penance and prayer.

"The Church became a live and open prayer community. Many pray every day for hours, in deep concentration. Common prayer in the families is again alive. The pilgrims meet the families in Medjugorje and renew their own private and common prayer. Around the altar at holy Mass and Communion, the faithful gather from the divided diocese and pray together for the diocese, the priests, and for the whole Church.

"Through practical faith, the role of Mary here is deeply expressed as the Mother of the Church and Mediatrix of all graces. The Church becomes the Church of peace because individuals, families and communities reconcile with each other. In the prayer plan of the local church in Medjugorje, the great needs of the whole Church, and the Church in our nation, always come first."

At the end they state: "From all sides a multitude of people streams here daily. Without advertising or cheap propaganda, we have a church and consecrated area that is the most frequented in our country. . . . Here is felt a fresh wave of prayer and penance that is impossible to find today in this form, in any great shrine in the world. . . .Therefore, we invite you openly and brotherly, that we should together think about the experiences of the faithful here, and about the chance Our Lord still offers to our Church. Here God imposes Himself on His people to accept Him."

At the end they propose a call to all priests, for reconciliation and for daily prayer and fasting every week for this intention, and a call to the people for prayer and fasting for the same intention. Concrete programs are suggested for a closer relationship among the clergy and for the clergy's spiritual renewal. The group of priests should meet once a month for a spiritual renewal. Suggested are themes for meditation during the spiritual renewals, prayer, creation of good will, conversion.

Glas Koncila ("The Voice of the Council") in the May 1, 1983 issue, had a short report about it entitled "Medjugorje—Call for Prayer and Reconciliation."

"In the Year of Redemption, in the church of Medjugorje, all kneel and pray together every day, five Our Father's, Hail Mary's and Glory Be's in honor of Christ's suffering, and a sixth Our Father for the intentions of the Holy Father. Priests from Medjugorje call all worshippers of the Queen of Peace and all of the faithful and people of good will to join them in this celebration of the Year of Redemption, and to kneel in front of the crucifix every day and pray these prayers. Five Our Father's, Hail Mary's and Glory Be's in honor of the Passion of Jesus and one Our Father for the intentions of the Holy Father. In addition, they call for one hour of adoration to Jesus in the Blessed Sacrament on Thursday evenings in the church, or at home if it is not possible in the church, and one hour of adoration to the Holy Cross on Fridays, if possible at the same time it is held in Medjugorje. Both adorations, on Thursday and Friday, have been held in Medjugorje regularly."

NEWS FROM MEDJUGORJE DURING 1983

On the second anniversary of the apparitions, again there was a multitude of people in Medjugorje. On the day before the unofficial feast day of the Queen of Peace, June 24, there were more pilgrims than a year ago. Prayers and singing continued through the night. Some found a place on the benches in the church and slept there as much as they could, and others slept on the ground around the church. The weather at this time was pleasantly warm, not as hot and humid as the year before. All the hotels in the surrounding areas were full, but for the number of pilgrims there were not enough rooms.

The Franciscans in Medjugorje estimate that on June 25 in the afternoon and evening, there were one third more faithful than last year. Some believe that the number was doubled. There must have been 150,000 or more. It is not possible to have exact data. Many pilgrims came by ' bus. There was a great number of people from foreign countries. In the evening when all the celebrations in the church came to an end, it took over three hours for all the cars and buses to start moving.

On June 24 there were guards placed on both hills, Crnica and Krizevac, to prevent pilgrims access to the hills. The Franciscans were again ordered directly by the government, as before on similar occasions, to discourage people from climbing the hills, and they did so. However, by order of "higher authorities" the guards were removed that same day and everyone who wished to do so could climb both hills without any hindrance. A great many people took advantage of this and visited the places of the first apparitions on the hill Crnica. Since then, anyone and everyone has had free access to both hills.

On Sunday, September 11, there was a magnificent celebration around the concrete cross on the hill Krizevac above Medjugorje. It was the 50th anniversary, the golden jubilee for that symbol of our Redemption, that stands on top of this hill. Because of the prayers and sacrifices of the faithful who built the cross and all those who have climbed to it to present their prayers, sacrifices and penances to Jesus and Our Lady, this cross has become the spring of God's blessings and graces, not only for Medjugorje but for the whole nation and in a way, for the whole world.

Glas Koncila ("Voice of the Council") No. 19, September 25, 1983, reports that there were pilgrims in Medjugorje from Austria, Germany, Italy, France, Portugal, the United States of America, Canada, Argentina and Australia. Groups from Fatima and Milan, and a group of Croatians from Gradisce, Austria were specially mentioned. "It was a meeting of people with one heart and one soul, people from every race, language and culture who gathered without an invitation and unconditionally became brothers." It mentions the number as 120,000 pilgrims. The Franciscans estimate it as 150,000.

Two days later on September 13, through Jelena Vasilj, Our Lady sent a special message to the villagers of Medjugorje. She thanked everyone for every cup of water and every piece of bread and for everything they have given to the pilgrims, and also for the successful order and peace.

In the spring, Vicka was sick again; she was much weaker. She was examined by physicians, but they could not establish what was actually wrong with her. Just as before, she did not allow the other visionaries to ask Our Lady to heal her. At the end of July she had a tonsil operation. The operation was complicated but successful. She recovered quickly after the operation.

The duration of the apparitions of Our Lady in the small chapel in the church vary considerably. For example on July 11, 1983 the apparition lasted 39 minutes. After that, for a long period of time, the apparitions lasted longer than before. The seers say that Our Lady talks to each one at the same time, but to each one something different and only for him or her, and there is nothing about which they could or would be permitted to talk about.

In June, Our Lady finished talking about her life to Ivan and Ivanka. For Maria, she finished her biography sometime in July, and to Vicka she was telling her biography until April, 1985. The seers do not know when they will be allowed to make it public.

While Ivan was in the seminary in Dubrovnik, sometime during Lent he was taken to Heaven, as Vicka and Jakov were taken before (in the fall, 1981). He experienced an apparition of Our Lady before dinner. Our Lady invited him to come with her to Paradise. He was afraid, but went with her anyway. Just at that time, some of his friends were looking for him, but they didn't find him until he returned from his trip to Paradise.

Maria Pavlovic finished her schooling as a hairdresser and since then lives mostly at home. Since Vicka is not in too much contact with the pilgrims because of her illness, Maria takes over this role more and more. She receives the pilgrims, prays with them and explains the messages of Our Lady.

The former pastor of Medjugorje, Fr. Jozo Zovko, was released from prison on February 17, 1983, exactly 18 months after his arrest. After that, he was in Medjugorje until mid April, then was transferred as pastor in Gorica by Imotski. In the middle of August he was again transferred, as assistant pastor in Bukovica by Duvno, where he stayed longer, but was later transferred again as assistant pastor at Tihaljina close to Grud.

Jakov's mother died on September 5, 1983. She was sick for more than a year, but did not want to go to a doctor. She received the Sacraments the day before she died. Jakov is now with his aunt and uncle in the same neighborhood and they take care of him. When questioned whether Our Lady showed him his mother, he said that she did not, but she told him not to worry about his mother. Soon after, his father died too. (His father was living in Germany.)

During the summer two distinguished Moslems came to Medjugorje as pilgrims. One was the "Imam" (Moslem priest) from Blagaj. The Imam, an honorable person and evidently a sincere and deep believer, gave the following statement as the answer to questions from newspaper men: "Here, the people seek God. Whoever seeks God will find Him. Whoever finds Him will fall in love with Him. Whoever is in love with God, no one and nothing can ever make him unhappy."

At a novena before the feast day of the Immaculate Conception, Our Lady requested that the hymn to the Holy Spirit,

"Oh come Creator, Holy Spirit" be sung daily. The people sang that hymn daily, every evening until Christmas. Then one of the visionaries said that Our Lady would like them to pray this hymn every day. Since then, every evening before the Mass, the priest prays and the people repeat after every verse, "Oh come Creator, Holy Spirit!" Before that, the priest invites all the faithful who do not speak Croatian, to repeat in Latin, "Veni, Creator Spiritus!"

LET US CONTEMPLATE A LITTLE!

If someone asked why Our Lady expressly selected Hercegovina and Medjugorje for her apparitions, I think the answer would not be hard. If someone only passed through Hercegovina he would have to notice how many newly built churches there are, as the fruit of the calluses, sacrifices and denials of the people who live there. It is a proof of their faith, their Christian life, in spite of all their imperfections. And the church in Medjugorje is the largest of the churches built in recent times. Is it then a wonder that Our Lady came here?

The people, as people everywhere, were often and in many ways disloyal and inconsistent in their faith. There were all kinds of sin and scandal. But here something happened that could hardly be imagined any place else on earth. Eight days after the beginning of the apparitions, the seers testified publicly in the church about seeing Our Lady and they transferred her messages to the people. And at the same moment everyone believed and accepted Our Lady and her messages and as by a plebiscite, took upon themselves the obligation of strict fasting. This was not only a conversion of the entire parish, but had spread much farther outside the boundaries of the parish instantly. This conversion and fundamental change in the lives of innumerable people still goes on, even after a long period of time, and it has become even more intense and spreads more and more not only in Yugoslavia, but throughout the world.

A German pastor came to Medjugorje as a pilgrim in the

fall of 1983 and later stated: "Here, people finally have time for God again!" An excellent remark! It is perhaps the greatest shortcoming of our time, that people have time for everything and anything. But for their God, they do not have time. And now, Our Lady comes, grasping them with the power and grace of God's Spirit and people suddenly have time for God. No one is in a hurry in Medjugorje. Holy Mass and sermons are long. Prayers are long and persevering, every day, every evening, for several hours. Every evening, a good portion of the people present are from the parish of Medjugorje, which now lives a completely new life. People pray much, not only in church, but also at home. They pray and fast as they have not done for centuries. Their faith is truly sincere, deep, and a strong factor in their lives. In places that are a great distance outside of Medjugorje and Hercegovina, even outside the borders of our country, the fresh breeze from Medjugorje can be felt. It brings refreshment and rebirth.

Our Lady certainly has her reasons to talk so much about prayer in her apparitions. The Franciscans in Medjugorje realized that, and they too talk much about prayer. Here are some of their thoughts. Fr. Tomislav Vlasic once said, "By prayer we can change God's plans!" Truly, we do not even surmise what power our prayer might have and what we can accomplish with it. Our Lady says, *Everything!* Of course we cannot change God's plans in an absolute sense, but we can, just as certainly, in a way "force" God to give up, to divert from us, from the world, from mankind, the evil by which we have been threatened. The Holy Scripture gives us many examples of such successful prayer. If Abraham would have found a certain number of praying people, God was willing to spare Sodom and Gomorrah. Because of Moses' prayers, several times God had given up the punishment that He intended to send to the people, and even destroy them. Because of conversion, penance and prayer, God had spared Niniveh...

Fr. Slavko Barbaric said in a sermon: "To pray means first to give." To give God our trust, our faith with which we will be able, according to Christ's words, to "move mountains" (*Mk.* 11:23). Only then can we receive from Him what we pray for. It is similar to holy Mass; first we must offer God bread and wine, and then in return He gives us the priceless gift of the Body and Blood of the Son of God. Without a doubt, failure of our prayer often has its roots in the fact that we, in our prayer, bring nothing to God, neither faith, hope or trust.

> Fr. Jozo Zovko once expressed the thought: "It is an illusion to defend peace with weapons. Weapons do not win wars. It is always only an untruthful, apparent peace. True peace comes from the heart that has converted to God. Prayers win wars. In a way, God needed Moses' arms raised and extended in prayer, while he prayed during the battle his people fought. When his arms were raised, his people were winning. When his arms were lowered, the people lost. From history we know many examples in which weaker armies, supported by an army of those who prayed, conquered much stronger enemies."

Our Lady obviously found good and authentic interpreters of her messages!

THE TWO-THOUSANDTH BIRTHDAY OF OUR LADY

René Laurentin, a French priest and Mariologist, has written several books about Medjugorje. He was in Medjugorje on the Feast of the Annunciation, in March, 1984. In a conversation with the Franciscan fathers, he expressed the thought that now, around 1983-1985, should be about two thousand years from the birth of Our Lady. After a few days, the Franciscan fathers asked Our Lady, through Jelena, when her two thousandth birthday is. Our Lady answered that it will be her birthday when the whole world converts. Later she stated: *You asked for my birthday and I told you it would be when the world converts. You were not satisfied. I will tell you the day and you prepare yourselves.*

During the months of April and May Our Lady mentioned

her birthday several times. On April 24 she said to prepare for it with three days of prayer, also two days before it, and on the day of her birthday. Two days before should be preparation days with prayer and penance, and on her birthday we should not work but only pray. She added: *There will be many conversions. This day is a special gift from my Son to console me.*

She did not say the exact date right away but only that we will be told and to get ready. On May 25 she told the exact date; two thousand years from her birth was August 5, 1984. The Franciscans immediately informed the Bishop of Mostar, but he said it should not be talked or written about because no one could introduce new feast days without permission of the Holy Father. So the Franciscans did not make it public and did not write or talk about it. But people learned of it and prepared themselves. The Franciscans prepared the people by special prayers and penance, without mentioning the birthday. People in the parish and many others actually prepared themselves and many fasted on bread and water for nine days before the birthday. Many families did nothing but fast and pray for the three days before the birthday.

Sunday, August 5, 1984, the birthday of Our Lady, was truly a day of prayer. This was felt among the parishioners and among the pilgrims. Fr. Tomislav Vlasic said that he realized then, for the first time in his life, the meaning of the Lord's Day, when people spend the whole day in prayer and live that day in God, as opposed to our Sundays and feast days that became days of tourism. The graces could really be felt among the people. All the seers say that Our Lady was very happy on that day during the apparition.

The next day Our Lady said, through Jelena, *Continue praying and fasting and make me constantly happy as you did yesterday!*

Many pilgrims came for the birthday of Our Lady. Many stayed in Medjugorje for three or four days, especially on Saturday and Sunday. It was definitely more people than on the Feast of the Assumption. This gathering was the most beautiful and most spiritual that Medjugorje ever saw, even at the anniversary or on any other day. There were, of course, many foreigners, somewhat less than for the anniversary, but more people from France. Again, there were signs and an appearance of light on top of Krizevac and on the hill of the apparitions, which people could not only see, but watch for a long time.

All of the priests in Medjugorje, and all the priests who came to visit, experienced in these days, a special miracle. People confessed and were unbelievably open. They came from different regions simply to go to confession. Some were on their way to the sea for the weekend or for vacation, and a power simply pulled them to Medjugorje. Some who came had not been to confession for 20 or 30 years. The confessions were such that it was not necessary to search their souls or drag things out. It was as simple as at the time of John the Baptist. People asked, "What do I have to do, how can I better myself?"

DURING THE YEAR 1984

On her birthday, March 18th, Mirjana again experienced her meeting with Our Lady in Sarajevo, as Our Lady had promised. March 25, 1984, 33 months since the beginning of the apparitions, was the 1000th day of the apparitions. On that day the apparition took place in the sacristy of the parish church in Medjugorje, because the chapel where the apparitions usually occur was too full of those who wanted to be present at the apparition. One person who was present, said that at this apparition, the visionary Maria was extraordinarily beautiful, even more beautiful than Vicka becomes during apparitions. This does not usually happen. This time Our Lady said: *Rejoice with me and with my angels because a part of my plan has already materialized. Many have converted, but many do not convert at all. Pray...* And then she started to cry.

On April 24, 1984 Our Lady said through Jelena: *The world does not need information. The world knows what it must do. Many come to the church and when they hear the information about the apparitions they say, 'We are happy.' They return home and continue to live as they have lived before. Tell the people when they come that this is a place of prayer and they should pray.*

All that Our Lady says can be reduced to prayer, fasting, penance and conversion. Everything else is only an incentive to turn in this direction.

People who come to Medjugorje, particularly newspaper people, are interested in outside events. But all of the events, everything that happens in Medjugorje, are events of grace, inner events, events of an inner direction. The most important events occur *inside of people.*

On the third anniversary of the apparitions there were again more people than the year before. June 24, 1984 was a Sunday and many more pilgrims came than the pevious year. There were a relatively large number of foreigners, mostly Italians, about two thousand people. There were also approximately three hundred French, German, English and others. There were many priests, about 180. The message of Our Lady for that day was, *Children, I thank you for every sacrifice you have made on these days. Convert, reconcile, fast, pray, pray, pray!*

The number of pilgrims is constantly growing, particularly the number of foreign pilgrims, especially Italians who come in great numbers. They are there every day. At every step you can hear the Italian language. Pilgrims also come from other countries, even from across the sea.

On Sunday, after Mary's Feast day on September 8, 1984, there was again a big celebration at the cross on Krizevac. It was a beautiful day. Pilgrims came from all parts of the world; from America, Belgium, France, not to mention the Italians.

It must be stressed that this year (1984) Krizevac was completely included in the Eucharistic Congress in Marija Bistrica. All 13 evenings before the Congress, the Franciscans in Medjugorje followed the program of preparation for the Congress. Every evening 1,500 to 3,000 people participated. On August 5, Fr. Vlasic invited the pilgrims to pray a part of the rosary every day for the success of the Eucharistic Congress. In the Mass and in the sermon, Medjugorje was simply included in the community in Marija Bistrica, meditating in particular on the happenings there.

There was such a big crowd on Krizevac in the area around the cross that it was impossible to pass through and distribute Holy Communion. Confessions were impossible. On Krizevac, the lack of priests was felt.

Many priests went to Marija Bistrica and others were busy in their own churches. That afternoon, the priests offered their services to the pilgrims around the church and many people went to confession. Many from the crowd on the hill remained for the evening Mass.

On Krizevac too, a deeper piety was felt this year. During the three years of climbing the hill, people got used to praying while climbing. A whole stream of people prayed while climbing the hill. There were also prayers at the top. All together, it lasted about two and a half hours; first the rosary, then the Mass, then prayers and the consecration to the Sacred Heart of Jesus. This was all finished within an hour, but it took two hours for the people to come down from the hill to the first houses in the village.

The Franciscans from Medjugorje informed the Pope several times, in detail, about the events in Medjugorje, about the messages of Our Lady, and particularly about the 2000th birthday of Our Lady.

In the beginning of September, Fr. Tomislav Vlasic was transferred from Medjugorje to Vitina by Ljubuski, 25 kilometers from Medjugorje, as an assistant pastor.

PHYSICIANS TEST THE SEERS

A group of French physicians from Montpellier visited Medjugorje three times in 1984 and examined the seers from a medical point of view. That was on June 9th and 10th, October 6th and 7th and December 28th and 29th. They came for the first time on June 9th. About three hours before the apparition they met three seers; Ivanka, Maria and Jakov. They told the children that they intended to examine them. Jakov emphatically stated in the name of all of them: "Our Lady said that this is not necessary!" The physicians answered: "It is not necessary to you or to the ones that believe, but it is useful to the ones who do not believe, and even to the bishop who thinks it is a hallucination or a dream. The electroencephalogram eliminates these doubts. To refuse the test would mean that you are afraid of their results. . ." Jakov ended the conversation: "Good, we will ask her tonight. . ."

His refusal was so resolute that the physicians expected a negative answer. Therefore, they were greatly surprised when on the same evening, after the apparition, Jakov came, all smiling and immediately said, "Our Lady answered, It was good that you asked me, you can take the tests."

The physicians came with all the necessary technical equipment. On the first visit they took Ivan's encephalogram (the rhythm of the brain's activity) before, during and after the apparition. On the second visit they took the encephalogram of Maria and Ivanka, and they took Vicka's and Ivanka's blood pressure and electrocardiogram (rhythm of the heart). They made eye tests of all four seers. During the third visit they examined the sight, hearing and functioning of their voice and throats.

The bishop of Mostar, Msgr. Zanic, stated that the tests of these physicians were not necessary for him. The physicians from his Commission did not make a single encephalogram or any medical test during the apparitions.

The results of these tests can be stated, in short, as follows:

> "All the findings show that these young people are normal and healthy in body and mind. Epilipsy is definitely not present, nor are their experiences dreams or any kinds of hallucinations. There is no hysteria nor catalepsia (stiffness, paralysis). The ecstasy of the seers is not pathological and there could not be any deceit."

Thus, these findings exclude the presumption that this may be a collective hallucination.

Descriptions of these results are published in a separate book: Prof. H. Joyeux—Abbe R. Laurentin: "Scientific and Medical Studies on the Apparitions at Medjugorje" (English edition first published in 1987 by Veritas Publications, Dublin, Ireland.)

THE YEAR 1985

The stream of pilgrims is growing more and more. Pilgrims from foreign countries, especially Italians, are coming in growing numbers. All the hotel rooms in the surrounding areas are reserved far in advance. Many pilgrims find lodging in the villages which finally obtained running water. However, because of large quantities of water used, sometimes there is no water. Still it is much easier than before, when people could drink only from the cisterns, which was not enough for the increased usage of water due to the pilgrims. At the anniversary celebration (1985), 80 priests concelebrated the Holy Mass (and sometimes there are even more). At the anniversary, Fr. Tomislav Ivancic, from Zagreb, celebrated the Mass and gave a sermon.

A group of twelve Italian physicians and a Church expert for apparitions came with all their technical instruments and filmed all four seers and talked with them from the 7th to the 9th of September. Four physicians from one of our clinics joined them in their work.

Last winter, television from Ljubljana made a documentary film about the events in Medjugorje and showed the film on April 24, 1985. On the Feast of the Assumption, television from Belgrade made an even better documentary film which was aired on October 15, 1985 as part of the show "Kino-oko." Television in Sarajevo did not show that film even though it usually airs the programs of "Kino-oko."

It was now forbidden for the visionaries to have apparitions in the chapel in the church, and therefore, since Easter, the apparitions occured every evening in a room of the parish house. Vicka is often ill and has to stay in bed. Thus she does not come to the apparitions with the others. However, even when she is in great pain during the day, in the evening at the usual time, she gets up and apparently completely refreshed, experiences the apparition in her home and receives Holy Communion before or after, whenever it is possible for the priests to bring it to her.

This year, among the pilgrims, there were some bishops, one each from Poland, Germany, Brazil, Zaire and Thailand

and an Orthodox bishop from France.

After the apparition, the visionaries always pray the song of Our Lady, *Magnificat* ("My Soul Magnifies the Lord. . ."). The seer, Ivan, tells how this came about: "When we come home in the evening after the Mass, we pray the Glorious mysteries of the rosary in front of the Crucifix. Then we take the Bible and meditate on one part of it. Once we were attracted to the Magnificat. This is a song of thanksgiving, the canticle of Our Lady. And we felt the need to say that prayer. Now we pray it after every apparition; it has become a dear habit."

THE YEAR 1986

The number of pilgrims continues to grow. Italians prevail numerically, but there were days when most pilgrims were talking German or English. Slovenians came several times by a special train from Ljubljana. The Irish come regularly by charter planes in groups of about 120 pilgrims. Only small groups come from Latin America which is understandable because of the great distance and the poverty of the population. There were several groups organized from Africa. Copts came from Egypt with two of their bishops. Pilgrims also came from countries in Asia. The faithful come from almost all Christian communities, even from the Far East and the American West. Budhists and Moslems also come. The great majority come to sincerely meet God, because they feel that they are lost.

The parish office sent several written requests to the authorities to sell them a half demolished building on the western side of the church, together with its yard. A long time ago that building was the school of the congregation of the School of Sisters of the Third Order of St. Francis. After the war the building was confiscated but still served as a school building. It has not been repaired, and a few years ago it was completely abandoned when a new school was built. The authorities at first did not even answer the request, but in the spring of 1986 the request was denied with the explanation that society does not have any interest for this building and its yard.

Fr. Ivan Dugandzic said: "It was very hard for us when, a few weeks after that, a group from Citluk came and started to measure the yard in front of that old house. They distributed the area to all kinds of merchants from Zenica, Sarajevo, Sabac and Pozarevac. Many brought their whole families with them, set up tents and made their homes there. When a group came from Sarajevo to plan merchandising in that area, a woman from that group said to me, 'This is terrible.' "

Thus, the commercialization has begun and is spreading quickly, unfortunately without plans, and is very ugly. It is still a big problem to find shelter for foreign pilgrims. A sewage system has been set up but it is often closed and access to it is difficult because of the many merchants.

THE YEAR 1987

Glas Koncila ("The Voice of the Council") No. 27, from July 15, 1987 carried an editorial under the title, "Commentary: Fatima and Medjugorje in Marian Year." At the end of the article it says: "According to the various European pilgrim and tourist agencies, it seems that a great many of those devoted to Mary from different countries will go to Medjugorje, especially since this is the Marian Year. The Yugoslav state authorities are not disturbed any more because of this fact, since they have learned to differentiate very well between the belief or unbelief in the apparitions of Mary and the giving of concrete service concerning the traffic, shelter, food and other civil help to the pilgrims of Mary. Our local Church should, however, because of publicly announced but insufficiently clear standpoints, ignore the whole phenomenon, if not prevent it. Perhaps the whole situation could be solved if our bishops would publicly and strictly distinguish between the two sides of the Medjugorje problem: the question of the apparitions and the question of the massive gathering of the faithful in a church of Mary, or rather around it. In that case, the first question could remain with no rush on the study of experts, and the second question would be accepted as a fact, in the reality of our Church, and to be responsibly controlled and directed. . . ."

In the same issue of *Glas Koncila,* the article "International Medjugorje" contains a report about the celebration of the sixth anniversary of the apparitions.

> "Pilgrims pray and sing in all languages of the world. For two hours they climb the rocks on Krizevac or kneel on sharp stones above Bijakovici. . .Hundreds of thousands pass through Medjugorje, not disturbing the atmosphere of peace, piety and prayer. . ."

On Thursday, June 25th, many pilgrims from the whole world came to Medjugorje. Our radio and television reported about half a million people. Among the honored guests was René Laurentin, Mariologist of world fame, the wife of the president of the Republic of Ireland, the mother-in-law of the president of the Philippines, as well as many Irish people, Italians, Germans, Spaniards, and Brazilians.

Hungarians came in a group of over 2,000; the whole world was on the rocks of Hercegovina. Medjugorje is truly an international prayer center. The night before, they say there was not a stone where a foot could stand. The prayer and silence were disturbed only by the helicopter that flew above the hill. Two local television crews, a German crew and an American cable television crew stayed in Medjugorje for days. Recently some Masses have often been celebrated in Arabic because there are many pilgrims from Egypt.

In front of the church there is now a park (where benches stood previously) and the ground is covered with flag stones. In the center of the park is a beautiful statue of Our Lady made of white Carrara marble. The statue is a gift of a Swiss man and it was made by an Italian sculptor. The pilgrims walk around the statue with the rosary in their hands, many walking on their knees, praying loudly and singing Marian songs. In the park in front of the church is also a fountain for the convenience of thirsty pilgrims.

In Medjugorje and the nearby villages, new homes are being built, and small hotels and restaurants. It is easy to get a building permit, only the Franciscans are forbidden to build a new parish house. And not only are they unable to give shelter to the great number of priests who hold confessions day and night, but the Franciscans of Medjugorje sleep in the church tower. In spite of many merchants close to the church, in Medjugorje you find silence, concentration and piety. Neither in restaurants nor by the half-dressed gypsies who sell junk, is there loud music or noise. Medjugorje has become an international center for praying. . .

The feast of the Assumption was celebrated as never before. An enormous number of pilgrims came from all sides. The celebration of the Holy Cross, on Sunday, September 13 was celebrated as usual with the same crowd of people.

It can be seen how many more pilgrims there were this year from the following comparison: In April 1986, about 55,000 Holy Communion hosts were distributed, and this year in April, there were about 90,000 distributed.

At the beginning of August the visionaries were forbidden to have the apparitions in the parish house. Since that time, the seers have their regular meetings with Our Lady in the choir loft of the parish church, out of sight of the faithful and pilgrims. The apparitions occur during the recitation of the rosary in the church before the Holy Mass.

PART THREE

MOTHER AND EDUCATOR

EACH SEER HAS A ROLE AND ASSIGNMENT

The apparitions are now in their sixth year. Those years have brought a great change in the life of the entire parish, but you can say with certainty that the greatest change occurred in the lives, behavior and attitudes of the visionaries. By their nature, they are very different. There are great differences in their characters, abilities, inclinations and many other things. On that natural basis, the grace that they continuously receive through the apparitions of Our Lady, continues to build and it creates truly great results. It has become more and more evident how every seer has a specifically determined role and assignment that he or she can and must accomplish, now and later, so that all of God's plans that He has for each of them can be materialized.

Virtually with every day it becomes more clear that the great graces and gifts that were given to them have been received so that God could influence others through them. Thus they should become the mediators of Our Lady's messages and of graces for many others. In all of this, they are constantly progressing and are becoming more and more mature. Of course, we can only guess a small part of that which they hide inside themselves. Their personal spiritual life, for the most part, remains hidden from us. But the fruits are visible, and awaken in us more and more, enchantment and gratitude to God who creates such deeds.

AND FOR IVANKA THE APPARITIONS CEASE

Ivanka Ivankovic was the first one who saw Our Lady and the first who talked to her. But she was the second one whom

Our Lady stopped appearing to regularly. Up to that point, Our Lady related to her, too, some things concerning the future of the world and the Church, or, to be exact, she told her about future events in one part of the world. Ivanka herself says that she cannot talk with anybody about this, until Our Lady gives her permission to do so. Our Lady started to tell her these happenings on July 9, 1983.

On May 6, 1985, a regular apparition occurred in a room of the parish house in Medjugorje. Present were the seers Maria, Jakov, Ivan and Ivanka. That evening something happened that never happened before. Before that, the apparition always started and stopped for all the visionaries at the same instant. On that evening, after the apparition of two minutes, Maria, Jakov and Ivan said "Gone!" (Ode), but Ivanka, independently from the others, remained in ecstasy six more minutes. Ivan continued to pray as if nothing unusual had happened. Maria admitted that she had been frightened because she did not know what was happening to Ivanka. For Maria, it was the first time to see someone else in ecstasy during the apparition. After the end of the apparition, Ivanka said that she received the tenth secret, that Our Lady finished her messages to her about the future of the world and the Church, and that Our Lady told her to stay at home tomorrow and wait for her.

On Tuesday, May 7, Ivanka was at home with her grandmother. She went to pray in her room and experienced the apparition which this time lasted about one hour. Our Lady asked her to offer her sadness (caused by the end of the apparitions) as a sacrifice for the conversion of the world. Ivanka wrote down the description of her last meeting with Our Lady, and gave it to Fr. Slavko Barbaric:

"As every day when Our Lady comes, she greeted me with 'Praise be Jesus!' and I answered, 'Forever Jesus and Mary!'

"I have never seen Mary as beautiful as on that evening. That day she was wearing the most beautiful dress that I had ever seen in my life. The dress was shining like silver and gold. Her veil and her crown shone the same way. There were two angels with her. They too were dressed in silver and gold. Our Lady was so beautiful—and the angels too—that I cannot describe it in words. This has to be experienced.

"Our Lady asked me what I would wish? And I asked to see my earthly mother.

"Our Lady smiled and nodded her head. Then suddenly my mother appeared. She was smiling. Our Lady told me to stand up. I stood up. My mother hugged me, kissed me and said: 'My child, I am so proud of you!' My mother kissed me again and disappeared. After that Our Lady told me:

My dear child, today is our last meeting. Do not be sad because I will come to you on every anniversary, except this year.

My child, do not think that you did something wrong and that therefore I will not come anymore. No, you did not. You have accepted with your whole heart the plans that my Son and I had and you have accomplished them. The grace that was given to you and your brothers and sisters, was not given to anyone else on this earth. Be happy because I am your mother who loves you with my whole heart. Ivanka, thank you for responding to the call of my Son and for persevering always at His side and staying as long as He asked of you.

My child, tell your friends that my Son and I are always with them when they call and seek us. Whatever I have told you during these years and the secrets I have revealed to you, for now, do not speak of them to anyone until I tell you.

"After these words, I asked Our Lady whether I could kiss her. She only nodded her head. I kissed her.

"I asked her to bless me. She blessed me, smiled and said: *Go in God's peace!* and she left slowly, and with her went the two angels.

"Our Lady was very happy. She stayed for one hour."

After that, Ivanka went to Vicka's family. She stayed there long and cried. She was quite depressed after the apparition. She begged them not to ask her much. For a long time she felt lonely. She seemed sad at first, but then she calmed down. She continued with the spiritual practices that she had followed through the last few years. She was present with Maria at a prayer seminar.

Her father, Ivan Ivankovic, said that he felt as if a member of his family had disappeared. Ivanka's family was very close to the apparitions of Our Lady that Ivanka had experienced.

According to the promise of Our Lady, on the anniversary of the apparitions (June 25, 1986), Ivanka experienced again the apparition in the house of her grandmother in Bijakovici, where she had her last regular apparition. Present were the members of her family and some pilgrims. Ivanka said the following about this apparition: "The Mother of God stayed with me for 14 minutes. She was very joyful. She would like to tell mankind now that prayer is most important. Then she talked to me about the secrets and finally personally to me. We prayed together the Our Father and the Glory Be. She blessed everybody who was present."

On the Sunday after Christmas 1986, Ivanka was married in the Church to a young man she "went with" for seven years, even before the apparitions began. She always said that she would marry him. It is interesting that it was Ivanka, who was in love and intended to marry—who first saw Our Lady and started to talk with her.

Our Lady did not forget her promise. On June 25, 1987, Ivanka had the promised meeting with Our Lady once again.

Our Lady also stayed this time for 14 minutes. Again she called for prayer and renewal of the faith. Ivanka says that Our Lady was especially joyful.

MIRJANA DRAGICEVIC

"...I changed very much. Above all, I realize now how empty my heart was before the apparitions. Now, I really feel God, the Mother of God and the Faith—and I see them completely differently. My relation toward the Mother of God became a relation of a daughter to her mother. And I look upon the dangerous situation of the world differently. Above all, I feel sorry for the young people. I believe that many of them never had an opportunity to know God. From the many young people I meet in the city (Sarajevo), I could hardly name two or three who really believe.

"When I look at Medjugorje, I feel that it was much more beautiful before than it is now. After a period of time, people have again fallen back in their religious life. In the first year of the apparitions, life was the most beautiful. Everybody went to the Holy Mass and they helped each other. And now, they all believe that the Mother of God is always here and that she will always remain here, as if she had always belonged to us. And thus, many think: 'If I cannot go to church today, I will go tomorrow.' People do not feel the pain of the Mother of God because of such negligence. I certainly have to state, too, that people in Medjugorje have been a great help to the six of us. Without their help we would not have been able to undertake anything. We would have been laughed at. . ." (*Medjugorje,* published by *Sveta Bastina,* Duvno 1986, page 44).

Fr. Petar Ljubicic, assistant pastor in Medjugorje, the priest to whom Mirjana confides, says about Mirjana:

". . .It could be said that Mirjana lives in an environment that is very far from the Christian spirit and life. She lives in a society for which God means little or nothing. She is in contact with young people who have lost meaning in their lives. Mirjana admits openly that she feels sorry for those people who are far away from God. They would certainly have an opportunity to see all that is happening in the world and therefore seek the meaning and goal of their life. However, these young people rejoice only in things that are worldly and passing. It seems to me that this experience helped Mirjana in many ways to give herself completely to God. She is therefore trying, from day to day, to dedicate her life to the conversion of this world.

"I noticed one thing in particular. Our Lady wants Mirjana to pray and make sacrifices for the conversion of the above mentioned unbelievers. This is, I think, the difference between Mirjana and the other visionaries who live here in Medjugorje. These five visionaries have around them here more or less a Christian spirit, while Mirjana has to live her conversion in an unbelieving environment.

"Concerning the secrets, Mirjana herself maintains that it seems to her that the day of their fulfillment is nearing. And right now, Our Lady calls her to work on a special program— what she has to pray, and how she has to live. At the same time she calls, through Mirjana, all people of good will to join Mirjana in prayer. God has announced that He will send us signs of advanced warning. By this, He wants to show clearly that He is forever the Master of this world! God will send advanced signs and some signs that will be lasting.

"Mirjana says: 'When the signs appear, many people will convert, many who have doubted until recently and pondered over whether what is happening in Medjugorje is coming from God or coming from some other side. To all who are open to God's Spirit, it will be clear that God is truly present here and dwells among us people.' " (*Medjugorje, Sveta Bastina,* Duvno 1986, pages 50-51).

As Our Lady had promised, Mirjana regularly has an apparition every year on her birthday, March 18, and then she sees Our Lady as she had seen her through a year and a half of regular apparitions. But during 1985 and 1986, Mirjana had more meetings with Our Lady. Sometimes, it was only an inner voice, the same voice of Our Lady which is so well known and dear to her. At other times, she had a visual apparition. On all of these occasions, Our Lady talked to her about the secrets that she will have to make public soon.

Fr. Petar Ljubicic makes it known that Mirjana selected him as the priest to whom she will tell the secrets that he will have to announce. Our Lady gave Mirjana a paper that looks like parchment, and which Mirjana will give to the priest ten days before the secrets occur. After one week of prayer and fasting, that is, three days before the secrets are to occur, he will be able to read the secret from that paper and announce it. The first two secrets will be advanced warnings and proof that Our Lady was here in Medjugorje. The third secret will be the visible sign promised to appear on the hill of the apparitions. (*Medjugorje, Sveta Bastina,* Duvno 1986, in the previously quoted article, and *Medjugorje, Gebetsaktion,* Wien 1986, No. 2, page 24).

On October 25, 1985, Mirjana had an extraordinary apparition. Fr. Petar Ljubicic was also present. Mirjana reports:
"Ten minutes before 2:00 P.M. we started to pray. Our Lady came and greeted me with *Praise be Jesus!* as always.

Immediately she started to talk about non-believers. She said that they, too, are her children, that she suffers because of them and that they do not know what is awaiting them. She was very sad and started to pray for them an Our Father and Glory Be. She said that most of our prayers must be for them.

"Then she prayed for the sick and the poor who are lonely. We also prayed with her the same prayer. Then she blessed us. After that, she showed me the first secret, as in a film. I was sad and asked her whether it had to be like that. She said:

"Yes! God is not hard of heart, but look around you. Who today still honors God, the Father, and prays to Him? How many people come into the church as in the house of God, with respect, strong faith and love for his Father?

"I could not answer anything.

"She said: *Very few.*

"Then she prayed two times in Latin over Fr. Petar. I was happy that she is satisfied with my choice of him. She said that his heart is completely open for God and he will be rewarded. . .Then followed one more Our Father and Glory Be for Fr. Petar that he could successfuly accomplish what was entrusted to him. Our Lady stayed with me about 8 minutes." (*Medjugorje, Gebetsaktion, Maria Konigin des Friedens,* Wien, 1986, No. 2, page 25).

"I cannot comprehend that I have experienced such a grace that I saw the dearest Mother for such a long time and that I spoke with her. When I think about Mary, about her most beautiful eyes, full of warmth, about her motherly hands, my soul is full of joy.

"Mary, how happy I was with you! Is there anything more difficult in life than losing something most dear to you? Dear Mother of God, you know best how hard it was for me in the beginning when I did not see you anymore. How happy I would have been if I had died at that moment. I cried and called you, dear Mother, repeatedly. But it was in vain. But now I understand that you only carry out God's plan. I thank you for the most beautiful time of my life that I was allowed to spend with you, my dearest Mother!

"I thank you for the pain I felt after you did not appear to me anymore. My good Mother, during that time, too, I felt your presence in my prayer. Dear Mother, help me! Fill me with the strength to tell people to whom they should pray and for what they should pray. Help me to tell them: You are our dearest Mother—so near to us all.

"Help me to tell them: Every prayer wipes away one tear that you shed for us. Help me so that I can say to them that you love them—all of them with the same motherly love.

"Not all had the good fortune to hear your beautiful voice and your pleas. Therefore, dear Mother, please, give me the grace that I can transfer it to people.

"It hurts me when I think that I can now see you only once a year. But I know that it must be like that. I courageously hold back my tears and pray, because I know that others do not have even that grace...

"I pray to you for unbelievers because of whom you suffer the most. Dear Mother, I will tell everybody and we will try together to dry your tears with our life." (*Medjugorje, Gebetsaktion,* Wien 1986, No. 4, page 22).

On January 28, 1987, Mirjana again had an apparition. At that time, Our Lady directed to all of us, through her, this particularly beautiful message which encompasses everything Our Lady has said in Medjugorje until now:

My dear children! I have come to you to lead you to a purity of soul, and with it toward God.

How did you receive me? At the beginning with disbelief, fear and mistrust toward the children whom I have selected.

Later, most of you accepted me in your hearts and started to carry out my motherly appeals. But, unfortunately, that did not last long.

Wherever I come, and my Son with me, Satan comes there too. You have allowed him to reign over you unnoticed and to direct you.

Sometimes you realize that some of your deeds are not permitted by God, but you quickly push that thought away.

Do not give in, my children! Wipe from my face

the tears I shed observing you in what you do. Look around you.

Find time to come to God, into the Church! Come to the house of your Father. Find time to gather together, and with your family, pray to God for grace.

Remember your dead. Make them happy with a Holy Mass.

Do not look with contempt on a beggar who begs for a piece of bread! Do not chase him away from your full table! Help him, and God will help you.

Perhaps the beggar's blessing that he gives you instead of thanking you, will materialize! Perhaps God will hear him!

All this, my children, you have forgotten. Satan helped you in it. Do not let him! Pray with me!

Do not fool yourself thinking I am good and my brother who lives next to me, is not good!

You will not be right. I, as your Mother, love you and therefore I warn you. The secrets are here, my children. It is not known what they are, but when you do learn, it will be too late!

Return to prayer! Nothing is more needed than prayer.

I wish that God would allow me to explain to you at least a little about the secrets, but even this is too many graces that He is giving.

Think about how much you offend Him! When was the last time you denied yourself something because of the Lord?

I will not scold you anymore but I want to call you once more to prayer, fasting and penance!

If you wish to receive a grace from God through fasting, nobody should know that you are fasting.

If you want to receive a grace from God, with a gift to a beggar, nobody should know, only you and the Lord!

Listen to me, my children!

In a prayer, think about these my messages!

VICKA IVANKOVIC

Each of the seers in Medjugorje has their own assignment, but it seems that this particular assignment is most noticeable with Vicka. With her, Our Lady has special plans and she carries them out loyally and conscientiously.

Fr. Janko Bubalo, in his book, *A Thousand Meetings With Our Lady in Medjugorje,* Jelsa, 1985, writes about his conversations with Vicka and about some of his observations and meditations. These conversations enable us to experience the Medjugorje events in an extraordinary, indeed three-dimensional way and so penetrate deeper into their essence and meaning that they have for all of us. In these conversations, Vicka unconscientiously gave us an extraordinary picture of herself. This picture is, of course, incomplete. It actually gives little concrete data; the greatest and most important could only be guessed. But the conversations reveal to us that Vicka has an extraordinarily rich nature. She has not only accepted the great graces of so many meetings with Our Lady, but has accepted them with her whole soul and being, and answered them with all the strength of her will and devotion.

Fr. Bubalo, in his book *Testimonies—Medjugorje, Blessed Land* (Jesla, 1986, pages 193-212) has included a detailed article about Vicka under the title: "The curtain is slowly opening." From this article, I am taking only the most significant parts:

"It is actually very difficult to talk about Vicka. That which is great and beautiful that she carries in herself, she skillfully hides, even from her closest ones. But, there is something that has already become quite evident—the vocation of her life is suffering. That in a completely unusual way, sets her, without any doubt, in the group of great mystics and sufferers. Her illness is not an ordinary human illness. She has accepted her suffering in advance, consciously and voluntarily, when she, in 1982, in response to Our Lady's offering of that suffering, said her great, 'Yes.' Nobody knows about it but Our Lady and Vicka...

"At the beginning, the suffering was only a slight headache and frequent fainting. In addition to this, there was the inflammation of joints which stopped after her tonsil operation. But then, the headaches and faintings became stronger. No one is able to truly understand as far as she is concerned. The rumors about her illness are even worse for her than the illness itself. Vicka often had examinations by physicians but they were completely unnecessary for her, and not at all useful. The longer the illness is lasting, becomes more and more difficult for her. The secret of her illness becomes all the clearer to her, but she keeps quiet. She does not talk about her illness even to her mother who worries very much because of Vicka's illness.

"On the evening of the seventh of December, she felt strong pains from the inflammation of her appendix. Her courage helped a little. The next day she was quickly taken by airplane to Zagreb and was operated on the same day. During the operation, Our Lady appeared to her and stayed with her to encourage and console her. The operation was difficult, because the appendix had already burst and there were some other complications. But, five days after, she was already home in Bijakovici.

"Vicka's suffering becomes stronger with time. Her faintings are always deeper and more difficult. Nobody can wake her from that condition but she regularly wakes up by herself, five or six minutes before the apparition which she now experiences every day at home with a few pilgrims present. Once, I was present at such an apparition. While a moment before she was in a deep coma, she comes cheerful and smiling as always, only somewhat pale, greets everybody and starts to pray with a strong voice, as always, before an apparition.

"The results of medical examinations are often published but they cannot identify the illness. She was given some multi-vitamin pills, only to give her something, but she did not take them. She gave them to a sick woman in the village. On October 20, 1984, a physician in Zagreb told her to fast less and rest more and solve all else with 'her Lady!'

"Vicka's illness is not usual but has a mystical character and is managed by God Himself, through the intercession of Our Lady. A proof of this is an event that happened on June 13, 1985. The day before, Vicka was in her deep coma all day long; she did not eat anything. Late that evening, she woke up from her "sleep" and went with a group to the hill for a nightly meeting with Our Lady. She returned around midnight and said to her mother that she would like to go to Humac, on a pilgrimage to St. Anthony. Her mother could not understand how she could endure it. But Vicka asked Our Lady (while on the hill), whether she could go to Humac. Our Lady said that she could go. At five o'clock in the morning, she was on her knees in front of a priest for confession. Everything went well and smooth. The next day, she was again, in a deep coma all day long.

"From January 7th until April 10, 1985, Vicka had been receiving Our Lady's biography during the apparitions. She took notes regularly and filled three big notebooks. On April 10th her meeting with Our Lady lasted very long. Our Lady told her then the name of the priest to whom she should later give those notebooks and he will take care of them. Vicka later told the priest about it and he quietly accepted the assignment. Nobody except Vicka and that priest know who he is.

"Vicka's suffering is great, but Our Lady has not abandoned her. It was very hard for Vicka that she was not able to participate with the others in the apparition in the church (or later in the parish house) but had to remain at home. Our Lady came to her regularly, and interestingly, during more than 15 months, Our Lady came every day at the second Our Father that Vicka prayed before the apparition, and always at the words: 'Thy will be done!'

"On September 17th, 1985, Vicka's mother waited for her to wake up from her coma for the evening apparition. When she woke up, her mother said, 'My daughter, why don't you ask Our Lady to at least shorten your troubles?' And Vicka told her: 'Mother, if you knew how many souls are benefiting from my doing this, you would not say anything.' Her mother then said: 'My daughter if that is so, it should be according to God's will.' Here, Vicka clearly revealed the reason of her suffering and the reason why she does not want to ask Our Lady to heal her, nor does she allow others to ask Our Lady for her health.

"On September 10th, 1984, a day after the celebration on

Krizevac, everybody who lives in the house with Vicka was present at the apparition. Vicka repeated loudly, several times during the apparition: 'Jesus, God!' Her sister Ana added to this every time: 'Have mercy on her.' But Vicka every time answered: 'No mercy.'

"From April 17th, 1985 until April 22nd, 1986, Our Lady talked to Vicka about the future of the world. Vicka again made notes and filled up two notebooks.

"Vicka's coma lasted up to 15 hours or more, on a given day, except when she had a "rest" as her sister Ana called it. That was, for example, for the birthday of Our Lady on August 5, 1985, for a full 8 days.

"Vicka never showed any fear because of her sufferings. She repeated several times that she does 'not fear life, and even less death. It should be God's will' For her, death is only a crossing from one house to the other, only from an uglier to a more beautiful one.

"January 3rd, 1986, around five o'clock in the afternoon, Vicka felt her coma coming again. This did not usually happen at that time. She was expecting to wake up on time for the apparition. However, she remained in a coma and at the regular time Our Lady came to her. Vicka found herself lying on her back. She folded her hands in her usual way and with burning face started her conversation with Our Lady. In a deep coma and talking with Our Lady! She did not wake up until around 10 o'clock at night!

"It had happened before that Our Lady appeared to her while she was in a coma. That could be noticed clearly by her looks and position, and sometimes she acknowledged it to someone in conversation. But until this day, it was never her regular 'official' meeting with Our Lady. Our Lady always appeared to her, in addition, at her regular time.

"The next day, on January 4th, everything was the same as the day before. Our Lady came to Vicka during her comatose condition and they talked again for 20 minutes. On the day before that, Our Lady offered Vicka a new triple task. Vicka was completely free to accept it or not, but she had to give Our Lady an answer by Sunday, January 5th, during the regular apparition.

"Vicka said that she was ready to immediately accept the proposal, but gave her answer on January 5th, as Our Lady wanted. That day, the apparition was attended by the titular bishop from Rome, Msgr. Paul Hnilica, along with a group of medical and other experts. They talked to Vicka before, but this time they found her in her comatose condition. With her mother present, they 'examined' her pulse, blood pressure, temperature and other data. Everything was normal, only Vicka did not give any sign of noticing what they were doing.

"Our Lady told Vicka that she would appear to her tomorrow, on January 6th, and then she would not come until February 25th. During that time, Vicka worked on her "triple" task. Except for Vicka, nobody knew what the task was about. She went alone on Krizevac and Podbrdo. During all these 50 days, Our Lady freed Vicka from her headache and coma because these symptoms were not compatible with her new task. She was asked whether it was hard for her to accept the proposal of Our Lady. Vicka answered, 'Not at all. I am indeed happy to contribute to Our Lady's plan.'

"She was happily awaiting her next meeting with Our Lady, which occurred together with Maria and Jakov in the parish house. At the moment of the apparition, Vicka looked unusually joyous. No wonder, after fifty days!

"Vicka was aware of the fact that now the headaches and coma would again continue. And they started on the last day of February. On the 23rd of February, Our Lady again gave Vicka a new assignment and announced to her that she would not appear to her until June 4th, a break of 40 days.

"Vicka had to have another operation. She went to Zagreb on May 27, 1986, hoping that now everything would be easier and that it all would be over by June, when she again expected a meeting with the Mother of God. But Our Lady wanted something different. The operation was not until June 7th, on the holy day of the Immaculate Heart of Mary.

"Our Lady did come on June 4th, as she had promised, but there was yet another surprise. Vicka expected Our Lady to come in the evening, at the usual time. Vicka was alone in the house of her relative and at noon she was preparing lunch. While she was cleaning something in the kitchen, suddenly something jerked her and she found herself in the room where Our Lady awaited her, though she did not take a single step nor did she open the door. As usual, Vicka fell to her knees and started to speak with Our Lady. The Mother of God was happy and congratulated Vicka and thanked her for the accomplished assignment.

"And that surprise, being against all expectations, should serve everyone as a clarification that the apparition of Our Lady is not an imagination or hallucination, but that Our Lady herself chooses the time and the manner of her appearing. The next evening, June 5, the apparition occurred at the regular time, as was the case on June 7th, while Vicka was in bed, immediately after the second operation. This time, they did not let Vicka go home immediately, but only after 11 days. At home, she had to stay in bed, too. And in such a position she met the Mother of God. On those first days, she did not have her usual headaches.

"Now, another trouble hit Vicka: difficult and long-lasting vomiting. She went to a doctor, but nobody could determine the cause. It was great torture for her but there was no help. The only joy was the meeting with Our Lady.

"On August 22, 1986, Our Lady gave Vicka the ninth secret. They said that Vicka started to cry after receiving the secret. The next day, August 23rd, there was again something unusual. Vicka spent the whole day with pilgrims but that day she had a strong headache. She could not stand it any more and went to her room. 'I don't like to be with people when I cannot rejoice in it!' She could not sleep, so she took the rosary, sat down and started to pray. She finished the Joyous Mysteries and—here comes Our Lady. Vicka was concerned that this was going to be her last apparition, but Our Lady gave her another assignment and said that she would not appear to her until October 20th.

"Vicka happily worked on her assignment. She went back and forth from Podbrdo to Krizevac. The headache appeared again. And so it went as she anxiously awaited October 20th. Because of a painful headache, and to prepare herself for the coming of Our Lady, Vicka retired to her small room after 3:00 o'clock in the afternoon. She started to pray with her sister Ana and then some pilgrims came, and they all prayed together. Suddenly Vicka noticed a triple flash, a sign that Our Lady was coming. She fell to her knees and the Mother of God was before her. Everybody noticed it and they too fell to their knees.

"Vicka was unusually joyous and Our Lady was, as rarely happened, 'festively' dressed. She congratulated Vicka and thanked her for again accomplishing her task enthusiastically.

"This was the last interruption, and since then Our Lady comes to Vicka every day, but now mainly in a new manner. She does not come at the usual time but unpredictably, between three and five in the afternoon. Vicka then wakes up from her coma but, after the apparition, quickly returns again to a comatose condition. Our Lady now usually stays with her longer than before."

Those three breaks in apparitions, Fr. Bubalo condenses in short like this: "Vicka had three breaks in the apparitions of Our Lady. All three times she was obligated to accomplish a task. All three times Our Lady told her the goal and the purpose of the task. All three times Our Lady congratulated her and thanked her for accomplishing the task. During the first interruption, Our Lady had completely freed her from the strange headache, and during the second and the third break, Vicka had some uneven headaches. After the third break, the headache became much stronger and long-lasting. Vicka said that, for her, the assignment during the second break was the most difficult."

Vicka will be permitted (she says) to soon tell at least someone what her assignments were and their purpose. She also knows how long her coma will last.

On February 4, 1988, Vicka sent the following note to Fr. Janko Bubalo: "Janko, here is what I had promised you: end of suffering—September 25, 1988. That is all. Many greetings from your little sister, Vicka." Fr. Bubalo received this note on the same day, read it and resealed it. He opened it again on September 25, 1988 before witnesses.

On Sunday, September 25, 1988 early in the morning, Vicka's suffering ended completely; her headaches, her states of unconsciousness, and everything else from which she had suffered for several years. Three days later, I spoke with her in her home in Bijakovici. She feels completely well. She comes to church for Mass every evening, and before the Mass, she has her apparition in the church choir loft along with the other visionaries. At the question whether or not she could now state the intentions for which Our Lady asked her to bear this suffering, she responded that for the time being, she was still not permitted to say anything about it.

MARIA PAVLOVIC

Maria is the visionary whom the pilgrims now almost continuously besiege. She receives large or small groups, first prays with them, then tells them, briefly, the messages of Our Lady. She is aware of the fact that this is God's will. For her, it is a great satisfaction that always gives her new strength so that she can accomplish what is God's will. She says:

> "I am deeply aware that, when it will be God's will today, tomorrow, when I die, I will certainly go to the Lord, Who will ask me about all that I did. And I really want to do as much as I can. From day to day, I feel that my thoughts are always directed toward Heaven. And, somehow, there is nothing on the earth that attracts me more. Because we are so often with Our Lady, and we would like to be with Our Lady, that we are truly ready without any hesitation to go, if Our Lady wanted, today or tomorrow, to Heaven. But in the same way, I know and I am aware of it, that Our Lady wishes me to be here, to work precisely here, to help the ones who are not aware of God's presence." (*Krsni Zavicaj*, No. 19/86 page 240: "The Joyous Testimony of Marija Pavlovic").

In October 1985, the Yugoslav television showed a movie about Medjugorje, in the program "Kino-Oko." There were reporters from Belgrade television on the grounds and they filmed everything, with some objectivity. Of all the visionaries,

Maria was noticed the most in the movie, simply because she was easiest to catch. She is usually home, surrounded with pilgrims. On the somewhat challenging question of a reporter: "Have you ever been in love with someone?" Maria answered perfectly calm and composed: "Yes, I have been for a long time in love with Jesus Christ!"

Janko Bubalo says that Maria is the most calm and ordinary of all six seers. She is plain on the outside, even though she is constantly in the center of attention. She is extremely simple and humble. On the inside she is "in love with Jesus Christ," all belonging to Mary. She offered herself completely, without limitations and exemptions, at the disposition of Our Lady for the materialization of her and God's plans. Slim and thin, she evidently fasts often, but is strong and has a strength for everybody. She has to help her parents and her brothers. In the morning they get up early and go to gather tobacco. Later they sort it. Then there are pilgrims coming all day long; she practically never has time for herself. When and how she finds time to pray and to live such an intensively spiritual life, is a secret between her and the grace of God and the grace of Our Lady. Anyone who sees her, cannot doubt the sincerity of her words and the truth of Our Lady's apparitions. The fruit of the graces and extraordinary working of the Holy Spirit are more than evident on her and in her.

Maria: "We await every day, with a special joy, the moment of apparition. Somehow everything else is not important. People come to us, we work normally, as everybody else. However, when it is fifteen minutes to six, that is the most beautiful moment of the day, and we wish for it more than anything else. We would like it best if Our Lady would take us to be always with her. . .

"The feeling that we have before the apparition, when we wait, we most certainly would not be able to describe to anyone, because others do not realize how great is our wish for the apparition, for the meeting. When Our Lady comes, it seems every time as something new, something more beautiful. The same is with Our Lady's face. Perhaps it is because we are growing and because we spend more and more time with Our Lady. We see that she is becoming more beautiful—as if we know her better now. . .

"Indeed, it can be seen by the face of Our Lady, how much we have grown, because we now realize more the greatness of Our Lady. She is certainly the same, but we experience her somewhat deeper. Just the thought, 'You are now with the Queen of Heaven and earth" makes you shiver in that moment because of all that grace God has given you. But, at the same time, you see such simplicity. . ." (*Krsni Zavicaj*, before indicated place, pages 238-239).

During the night from the 4th to the 5th of August, 1986, there was a large group on Mt. Podbrdo, about ten thousand or more. It was between 11 and 12 at night. After the rosary and an extraordinary apparition of Our Lady, Maria said to the people gathered there: "This evening Our Lady was very happy that we came in such a great number. I asked her for her blessing, to bless us all. Our Lady extended her arms and prayed over us for a while and then blessed all who were present with the sign of the cross. She said that she rejoices because we came in such a great number and because we dedicated our sacrifices to her. She thanked us for every sacrifice we made for Our Lady's intention and said that she loves us all and that she wishes that we all go home with one love and live her messages. She said that she loves with a special love, all of us who are here this evening." (*Testimonies—Medjugorje, the Blessed Land,* pages 216-217).

Once during her prayer, Maria Pavlovic saw a flower. The flower was closed, wilted, its head hanging as if it were dying. Then, a beautiful drop appeared above the flower and dropped on the head of the wilted flower. And the flower bloomed again and looked beautiful. Maria did not know how to explain this vision and asked Our Lady the meaning of it during an apparition on the hill. Mary said that the flower is a picture of the human soul. It blooms in the grace of God and wilts when the person sins. And the drop is a picture of the grace of God. If the person wilts with a sin, it blooms again when the person repents and goes to Confession. At the end, Our Lady told her that the Confession should be to her, and to others, a joy of the meeting with God. (*Testimonies—Medjugorje*, pages 218-219).

On July 21, 1987, Maria was asked how can we pray with our hearts, according to the wish of the Mother of God, while we are always so distracted. Maria answered: "We should simply give that time to God as a gift!"

IVAN DRAGICEVIC

After the beginning of the apparitions, Ivan suddenly decided on a vocation to become a priest and a Franciscan. He went to the seminary and there he experienced, and lived through great disappointments. As a seer, he was not understood and not acknowledged; only God knows how much and for what reason he suffered there. And the worst was he was not successful in his studies, and had to leave the seminary after a period of time. It was as if all hope was lost for him to fulfill his dream and wish.

It was only to Ivan that Our Lady offered to tell him his future. He was first reluctant but he accepted Our Lady's offer. What the Mother of God told him is his secret; he does not talk about it to anybody. But what is visible, shows that he has matured very much and has grown spiritually, as well as in his relation to others.

A separate prayer group of his friends and young people of his own age formed around him. It started in July 1982. At the beginning there were eight or nine, but by the spring of 1986, the number grew to 16. The objective of the group was to pray for world peace; to pray for the sick; the hungry and the poor, and to visit and help them. They pray for the intentions of Our Lady, and dedicate their sacrifices and fasting to her. They try to accomplish everything that Our Lady wishes. Our Lady leads the group through Ivan and gives them directions on what to do and how to do it. The group had its difficulties and problems of course, but with the help and leadership of Our Lady, they succeeded in overcoming them.

At the very beginning, when they were forbidden to go on the hill, the group had meetings in the field or in a house. Later, it became customary for them to go on Mondays to Podbrdo, to the place of the first apparitions, and on Fridays to Krizevac. Once a month, the group gathered in free and loose conversation of friendship and community.

On June 19, 1986, Ivan had to begin his civil duty and went into military service. He served his term in Ljubljana. He did not have regular apparitions there, but only on Saturdays and Sundays, when he left the army barracks. He returned from army duty June 13, 1987. His group met even while he was absent.

Now Ivan is again at home, with his group. When asked what his plans are for the future, he answers that Our Lady has her plans for him. And he is completely calm concerning his future.

JAKOV COLO

Since the fall of 1987, Jakov has been attending the second year of high school in Citluk. In general, he is seldom heard about, except that he has (with the other seers), regular meetings with Our Lady. Fr. Slavko Barbaric tells us that Jakov recently told him, that it is difficult for him to meet the school obligations on one side and at the same time to be at the disposition of the pilgrims.

The same priest also tells the following story:

A newspaperman from Vienna was present at an apparition and after it said to Jakov: "I do not have the impression that you experienced the apparition today. You seemed inattentive before and after the apparition. It seemed to me that you blinked your eyes during the apparition." Jakov said to him: "But in spite of that, I have experienced the apparition, just as the others." The newspaperman replied: "But I had the impression that you only pretended because the people were watching." Jakov remarked only: "And what shall I do, if you do not believe!" (*Medjugorje, Gebetsaktion*, Wien 1987, No. 7).

THE OTHER GROUP OF VISIONARIES

From the book *Medjugorje* (published by "Sveta Bastina," Duvno-1986), I am bringing here parts of the statements from Jelena and Marijana Vasilj—(*The Seers of the Second Generation*, pages 64-65).

Jelena: "It moved my heart mostly, and at the same time made me happy that I see the Mother of God as my own mother. I see Jesus as a friend or a brother, and God as my Father. They are so close to me, help me, and make me happy. It made me especially happy that God does not wish me to go away from my friends. He, indeed, wishes me to tell them and to show them with my prayer, what God means to me.

"Marijana and I see the Mother of God now every day. Before, it was three times a week and now Our Lady comes every day. Every time she announces her coming. She is dressed all in white and looks to us as a young girl, a young woman. Her cape and her veil are in one piece. She does not have a crown, but stars around her head. Her feet are covered by a cloud. Around her left hand she has a rosary. She is often very joyful, but also cries often. Recently, she cried very much. The angel whom I saw, looked like a little boy of about 12 years. Sometimes he looks like he is seven or eight years old.

"The voice that I heard is very hard to describe. In fact, I cannot describe it at all. Only, the voice of the angel, and the voice of the Mother of God, are different. Our Lady is to me like a mother, and the angel perhaps, as a brother who wants to show you how you can come to your Father. I often saw the angel. I saw him with the Mother of God and with Jesus and he was singing then. At the apparition on Krizevac I often saw six to seven angels. The angels are somehow all the same. But this cannot be described. If I try hard to remember, I have it exactly in front of me, but when I start talking, I simply do not find words for it.

"Our Lady has also shown me Jesus on the cross. I saw Jesus Resurrected. But, for me, it is somewhat different than for the other visionaries. I see the Mother of God somehow with my heart, and not with my eyes. Beforehand, I always pray very much. And then I see her when I close my eyes."

Marijana: "Our Lady introduced herself to us as the Mother of Goodness, Love and Mercy. She talks mostly about prayer—we must pray much—and about fast. Very often she also talks about peace that is so important for the world.

"Our Lady also talked about love. Once she said: 'Dear children, I am giving you very much love, but it depends on you how much you can take.' It seemed that those are the most important messages of the Mother of God."

Janko Bubalo condenses the differences between the first and the second group of visionaries: "From the observations so far, the following can be seen. Through the six seers from Bijakovici, Our Lady introduces herself as a sign to mankind, to whom a global, general call for salvation is directed. Through Jelena and Marijana, Our Lady leads to the depth of the spirit, explaining and helping them in their spiritual growth. Both sides are included in the program of Our Lady in Medjugorje." (*Medjugorje—the Blessed Land*, page 187).

Fr. Slavko Barbaric stated that: "The gift which Jelena received, came to being and is developing along with all the events occurring in Medjugorje. I dare say that this is the consequence of the happenings that began in June 1981. At the same time, this gift can be called a complementary gift of vision. After studying all the phenomena in Medjugorje, I would say that this gift 'needed' to be given, and is understandable in itself in the complex of the happenings.

"Let us try to differentiate: With the first group of visionaries. . .their visions do not depend on their personal prayer and fast, nor on their love for people with whom they live. Therefore, they received that gift "from the outside," without their own merit, by a free selection of God. The messages they transfer to us in the name of the Mother of God, they will understand as much as they will pray and fast themselves, but they could remain also completely superficial in transmitting the messages.

"Jelena Vasilj and the others around her. . .answered the call of the visionaries with personal prayer and fast. Jelena's gift could, in a way, be comprehended as the 'heart' of all events in Medjugorje, where there is talk about the awakening of the faith, and the prayer-penance spirit. Jelena transmits to us very simple messages, visions and directions.

"When everything is considered that we have heard so far through Jelena, then I can say that we are dealing here with a deep and concrete message, indeed. Not only Jelena's messages but also the conditions under which she hears and sees are a lesson for us. Jelena must pray, must love and forgive, must fast, to be able to 'hear and see'. She must personally live as the first person like that, so that the gift could be continued, develop and live in her. . . In her message, the following is also interesting. While the seers from the first group called the people and the parish community to prayer and conversion, Jelena maintains that Our Lady expressed the wish that they pray in prayer groups. . .

"I would especially like to add that the role of Marijana is the same as that of Jelena. For me personally, Marijana has become on the phenomenological level, an essential argument. Both girls help and support each other concerning the described charism. In this way, the danger is somehow diminished that one girl, for example, Jelena, will become too much the center of attention. The visionaries also find themselves in such danger." (*Medjugorje, Sveta Bastina,* pages 60-61).

During an inner conversation, Jelena asked Our Lady: "Why are you so beautiful?" She answered: *I am beautiful because I love. If you want to be beautiful, love!*

On another occasion, Marijana said to Our Lady: "Many told me today to bring you their greetings." Our Lady answered kindly: *Whenever one wants to greet me, he should pray the 'Angelus,' because that prayer is the most beautiful greeting for me!*

Since the fall of 1987, Jelena and Marijana both attend the second year of medical high school in Mostar. They travel there every day and return home the same day.

PRAYER GROUPS

Medjugorje is something unique in the entire history of the Catholic Church, and in the history of apparitions of the Mother of God. Thus, Vicka has a right to maintain that Our Lady appears in Medjugorje as she has never appeared before and will never appear anyplace else. (Bubalo: *Medjugorje—Blessed Land*, page 176). More than six years have passed from the beginning of the apparitions of Our Lady, and still, I am firmly convinced, none of us could ever guess, what God will accomplish and materialize through Our Lady in Medjugorje and through Medjugorje. Many things, however, already take some concrete forms. Here, we must first of all mention the prayer groups.

These groups are something completely extraordinary; something that has never existed anywhere in such a form. There were before, and still exist in the world today, many groups that are somewhat similar to the groups in Medjugorje, but it has never before happened that the Mother of God herself would form and lead such a group. In Medjugorje, there are mainly two such groups. They are very well described by Fr. Janko Bubalo (*Medjugorje—Blessed Land*, pages 176-198). Fr. Tomislav Vlasic also wrote something about the second of these groups. (*Medjugorje, Sveta Bastina*, pages 68-72). I will try to state here, something about these groups.

THE FIRST OR SMALLER GROUP

It originated spontaneously, actually during the first apparitions on Podbrdo. A group of young believers often gathered together in the evening, and then they would go to Podbrdo with at least one or more of the visionaries, to the place of apparitions. That happened all the time, even when it was forbidden to climb that hill. They would pray and sing there. When it was forbidden to be there, they prayed in low voices and gave up the singing. On such occasions, it often happened that the visionaries experienced an apparition of Our Lady, but not every time.

On July 4, 1982, there were five or six of them on the hill. Our Lady appeared, prayed with them, and determined the day and time for future meetings. At the beginning it was every Tuesday and Friday and later they switched from Tuesday to Monday. There was never more than 15 in the group. New members came, but some of the previous ones stopped coming. Our Lady requested from them that in the future, they be at her service with their prayers. From that day on, Our Lady appeared regularly at their meeting (of course, only to the visionaries), and through them talked to the group.

The requests of Our Lady were not always simple. The meetings were always at night, and some members live 30-40 kilometers from Medjugorje. It was necessary to come in bad weather and in the snow. But Our Lady gave them the strength for everything and filled them with great joy. Our Lady often invited them to pray and to make sacrifices for her intentions, but did not tell them what these intentions were.

In the beginning, they were alone at these meetings. Then other people found out (and pilgrims, too), and so many others came often to the meetings. For example, on the night from the 4th to the 5th of August, 1986, there were around ten thousand present.

These meetings do not have a strict agenda. Everything depends on what Our Lady suggests and on what the individuals feel as an inspiration. Several times Our Lady invited everyone present to express something. Some say that these are for them the most beautiful moments. Sometimes, they surprise themselves by the beauty and depth of this outpouring of hearts. They also write letters to Our Lady and, according to her wish, sometimes bring a flower which they give for her during the apparition.

The group is growing tremendously in cooperation and intensity in its spiritual life. It is obvious that Our Lady is preparing them for something special but it is not clear what this could be. All of them know many beautiful things that they have learned and experienced in Our Lady's school, but for now, they cannot talk about it.

Our Lady transmits her messages to the group during meetings with them on Podbrdo or Krizevac. There are always many more people present at those times as well. Sometimes up to ten thousand pilgrims or more. Our Lady usually prays over everyone present and blesses them. Here I would like to bring forth some of the messages that Our Lady gave in

August of 1988 because I find them particularly important and significant. Our Lady gave these messages through Ivan Dragicevic, through whom she leads this group.

My dear children, this evening my Son sent me among you. And I am happy with you. I am happy to see you in such a great number. I wish this joy to remain with you all day, and that you fulfill this joy with prayer as well. Live in happiness. I am also bestowing love upon you, that you live in love, and that you spread love. Your Mother loves you, and I am very happy this evening. I want your cooperation. I wish to work together with you, because your cooperation is important to me. I can do nothing without you. (August 4, 1988 on the eve of Our Lady's birthday, on Podbrdo. There were about five thousand pilgrims present, some believe there were even ten thousand.)

Dear children, your Mother is calling all of you this evening to pray for the youth of the whole world at this time. Pray, and through prayer renew yourselves at this time, preparing yourselves for the feast day. (August 8, 1988)

Dear children, your Mother is encouraging you to pray as much as you can these two days and that through this prayer, you prepare yourselves as much as possible for the upcoming feast day. Dear children, I wish to tell you to carry peace to others, to encourage others to change. You cannot spread peace, dear children, if you do not possess peace in yourselves. I am bestowing peace upon you this evening so that you may carry it to others. Be a light, dear children, that shines! (August 12, 1988)

Dear children, may a new year begin for you this evening— the year of the youth. In this year, pray for the young, talk with the young, because they are now in a very difficult situation. Help each other! I am thinking of you, dear children. May the youth of today play a role in the church. Pray, dear children! (August 15, 1988)

Dear children, I wish to tell you these days especially to pray for the young. I wish to send a message to my priests to organize and form their own groups through which they would instruct the young and give them true advice for their lives. And you, dear children, who are here tonight, you must be carriers of good words and peace to others, especially to the young. This evening, your Mother wishes to pray for all of you. (August 22, 1988)

Dear children, today I am calling you to give thanks to God the Creator. Give thanks for even the smallest things. Each one of you, every single day, give thanks for your family, for your place of work, for all those people that God placed on your way. (August 29, 1988 through Marija Pavlovic.)

THE SECOND GROUP

They call it the big or larger group. It came into being on the explicit wish from Our Lady. At the end of May 1983, Jelena Vasilj delivered to Fr. Tomislav Vlasic, Our Lady's wish that he be present at the apparition in her house. He came. After her prayer, Jelena had an apparition. Later she conveyed to him the wish of Our Lady. She wished that a group be formed that she herself would lead. Our Lady wishes that in the group there be young people, boys and girls, who are not obligated to work or bound by family ties and who want to consecrate themselves completely to God.

Our Lady requested that everyone who wished to participate in this group had to decide for himself or herself. She gave them one month's time to think about it. After that, everyone had to promise to pray, fast and accept sacrifices.

June 24, 1983 is considered the birthday of this group, because on that day Our Lady gave, through Jelena, directions, principles and rules for the group. Our Lady requests the following from them:

- To renounce all his or her disorderly passions, television, sports, smoking, overindulgence in food and drink, and so on.
- To completely surrender to God.
- To abandon forever any kind of fear. To someone who surrenders to God, in his or her heart, there is no more room

for fear. There will always be difficulties, but they will be to the honor of God and serve for their spiritual growth.

• To start loving their adversaries and enemies, not to carry in their hearts hatred, bitterness, judgments, but only love and forgiveness; to pray for their enemies and to bless them.

• To fast two times a week on bread and water. Our Lady also said that she will sometimes ask for fast three times a week if it becomes necessary. To come once a week to the meeting. Later, Our Lady asked to meet even twice and then also three times a week.

• To devote at least three hours a day to prayer, and of this, at least half an hour every morning and every evening. In the time of prayer, the Holy Mass and the Rosary are included. In the remaining time during the day, try to find free moments for prayer. Try to participate every day in the Holy Mass.

When they pray, they should not look at their watches—nor worry for their work—how and when they will finish it—because if there is worry, they will never finish it well. They have to give themselves up to the Spirit, to lead them into the depth. Then they will finish their work well and on time. For those who go to school or have a job, Our Lady asked at least half an hour of prayer every morning and every evening and that they participate at the Holy Mass, if possible.

They should not extinguish the Spirit of prayer, but use the free moments during the day to raise their minds to God.

Once, Our Lady said literally: *Pray, pray, pray! With prayer you can accomplish everything!*

They have to be careful because the devil tempts all those who decide to be completely consecrated to God. He will tempt them, too. He will tell them that they pray too much, fast too much, that they need entertainment as other boys and girls. They must not listen. They should listen to her, to the voice of Our Lady! And when they become strong in their faith, Satan will not be able to do anything to them.

They should pray much for their bishop and for the Church leaders. At least half of their prayers, they should dedicate to this.

Our Lady wishes that they consecrate themselves every day to the Sacred Heart of Jesus and the Immaculate Heart of Mary.

In the fall of that year, Our Lady expressed the wish that the members of the group commit themselves to her guidance for four years. She asked that, during that time, they not marry, not decide on a religious or any other vocation, nor make any permanent plan for their lives. She expressed a desire to lead the group deeper into prayer, and that afterwards, it would be easier for them to make an appropriate decision for their lives. She promised, that after four years, she would give them advice concerning their future lives. It was not clear what God's plans were for this group. But it is already clear that Our Lady called that group together to lead it herself in the depths of spiritual life, because she wants to prepare them for various roles in her plan. She wishes to give each member special assignments for special goals and graces for what she wishes to accomplish through the group.

The group has 38 members. Four are married, the others are not. Our Lady talks to them through Jelena and Marijana Vasilj. She teaches them about prayer, meditation, the Rosary, reading of the Holy Scriptures and about accomplishing the messages. She particularly stresses the reading of the Holy Scriptures. She told them how they should find God in all creatures in nature, and thank Him for all. The group has a retreat every year and, from time to time, more intensive meetings.

For a while, they were thinking that Our Lady would like to establish a new structure in the Church with this group (a new religious order or community). On such question, Our Lady answered: *My children, you do not know what you are asking. You do not know what is awaiting you. You cannot comprehend God's plans. I ask from you to do what I show you to do.*

In 1984, different branches were created from the large group, especially a small group that meets every day, and spends more time in common prayer. Through the visionaries, Our Lady gives that small group a special program which is becoming more and more intensive. Beautiful experiences occur in this group about which entire books could be written. For now it is not possible to talk about it, because Our Lady says it is too soon. In addition, many things concern deep experiences and the personal lives of individuals and only they should speak of it if they should feel that God urges them to do so.

Prayer is the most important factor in this group; prayer is actually everything. Our Lady teaches them and educates them in prayer, and through prayer.

The concept of prayer here encompasses fasting, giving up everything, penetrating all activities, by experiences in prayer. It is a yearning to always be with God and go deeper into Him. This is being in love with God. In addition, Our Lady requests from the group a weekly confession. She also educates them in cooperation. The members of the group are strongly bound together and by mutual sharing of experiences, they enrich each other.

I would like to state here my personal opinion that, with this group, Our Lady actually wishes to bring up saints who will be completely at her disposition, and through them, she intends to accomplish great deeds in the framework of God's plans. The time has passed when God could tolerate that we serve Him only half-way. The division of minds, that Christ announced in the Holy Scripture, will now be more explicit and determined. Our Lady said once that she can be patient with the people, but that she requests a change of life in persons consecrated to God, and in Church leaders. She repeatedly stresses and asks her selected ones to live in hope, to forever lose fear. And incessantly she calls for prayer: *Pray, pray to conquer Satan!*

Throughout the world, there are already many groups who wish to live, grow and develop by the model of this group in Medjugorje. For example, in Austria, there are already more than three hundred such groups. But none of them, anywhere else, can be exactly the same as this group in Medjugorje, because none of them was given by God what this group has, and that is, that Our Lady is present in the group and through Jelena and Marijana often talks to the group and gives explanations and concrete encouragements.

Here are some messages that Our Lady directed to the prayer group in Medjugorje:

January 27, 1986: *Every second of prayer is like a drop of dew that in the morning fully refreshes every flower, every blade of grass and speck of soil. In the same way, prayer refreshes man. When he is tired, he rests; when he is distracted, he again calms down. Man is renewed and is able to hear again the words of God.*

What a beautiful sight it is when we see fresh nature in the morning. The sight of man bringing peace, love and happiness to others is much, much more beautiful. If you could only know what prayer brings to man, especially personal prayer. A person can, through prayer, become a truly fresh flower for God.

You see, the drops of dew remain on the flowers until the first rays of sun come. Nature renews and refreshes itself in this manner. For the beauty of nature, it is necessary that it is daily renewed and refreshed.

Prayer refreshes man in the same way—it renews him and gives him strength. Temptations, that always return, weaken him and it is always again necessary that he, in prayer, again gets the strength of love and freshness.

Therefore, pray and rejoice in the freshness that God gives you. (Medjugorje, Gebetsaktion, No. 3, page 34).

November 8, 1986: *Dear children! Open your hearts and allow Jesus to lead you. To many that seems difficult, but it is so easy. You do not have to be afraid because you know that Jesus will never abandon you and you know that He leads you to salvation.* (Medjugorje, Gebatsaktion, No. 5, page 12).

March 1, 1987: *Dear children. You often overburden your hearts with some things that are not necessary. You are often afraid of this or that. Why is that necessary? The one who is with Jesus does not have to be afraid. Do not worry anxiously* what is going to come tomorrow or what will happen in a few years. *Give yourself to Jesus and only in this way will you become sheep who follow their shepherd.*

April 12, 1987: *If you love from the depth of your heart, you gain much. But if you hate, you lose much. Dear childen, love accomplishes great things. And the more love you have within you, the more you can love the people around you. Thus, pray constantly to Jesus to fill your hearts with love.*

May 16, 1987: *O children! Remember! The only way to be always with me and to know always what the will of the Father is, is to pray. Therefore, I call you today again, do not allow my calls to be useless. Try to pray through everything and you will understand the will of the Father, and love.*
Dear children! When God calls, it is a great event. Imagine how hard it would be to omit the chances that are offered to you. Do not delay until tomorrow or the day after tomorrow, but right at this moment say 'YES' to Jesus. And your 'YES' should be eternal.

June 16, 1987: *Dear children! My heart is full of graces and love. My heart is a gift that I am giving to you. Be united! Pray together! Love together!*

OUR LADY GIVES BLESSINGS

On September 15, 1987, I asked Maria Pavlovic whether or not some religious articles could be taken to Our Lady to have her bless them, now that the apparitions are so concealed. Marija replied: "Since it is now impossible to bring all the objects to the place of apparition, the seers ask Our Lady every evening at the apparition to bless all the objects that the faithful and the pilgrims have brought for that purpose. She does it always after the evening Mass in the Church, at the same time when the priest blesses these objects. Thus, at the same time with the blessing of the Church, Our Lady gives her blessing too."

In her message of July 18, 1985, Our Lady explicitly calls

us to have on our person blessed objects and at once adds why this is necessary:

Today I invite you to have in your houses as many blessed objects as possible; every person should have on his or her person some blessed object. Bless all the objects. Satan will then tempt you less because you will have a shield against him.

Since we are believers, it is clear to us that none of the blessed objects have some kind of magical power by themselves. We know that in addition, our faith and prayers are necessary, thus our personal participation. I can say for myself personally, with joy and respect, I always carry with me the Rosary that was blessed by Our Lady and pray on that Rosary. I also use the water that Our Lady in Medjugorje has blessed. And I can say that my prayers were fulfilled more than once. Those were indeed trifles, not big things, no miracles, but clearly granted prayers and help from Our Lady. Trifles can sometimes make our life miserable, and to the great God and to His and Our Mother, it is not hard to show us their love and care for us even through the small things in our lives.

PRAYER FOR THE SICK

Through Jelena Vasilj (on June 6, 1985), Our Lady gave us a special prayer for the sick and she wishes us to pray it over the sick and for the sick. I believe that sick persons themselves can and may pray it for themselves, changing, of course, the words depending on the situation.

My mother is old and sick and I pray that prayer for her every day though I am far away from her. I have to say that my mother experienced a considerable ease in her pains. Of course, this too, cannot be considered a miracle. It is not a miracle, but is, in any case, an answer to the prayer and an obvious help of Our Lady.

I would like to stress that this prayer has to be prayed perseveringly—as is true for all our prayers—just as we have to use the sacramentals and blessed objects persistently for their influence to be visible and useful. Persistency is always necessary for us and in all our prayers. God is not a waiter who must immediately jump when we ask for something. By the way, we have to wait for a waiter many times too! (The prayer for the sick can be found in the Appendix, at the end of this book.)

OUR LADY'S MESSAGES ON THURSDAYS

Our Lady has given us messages through her seers. These messages were particularly directed to the parishioners of the parish of Medjugorje. At the beginning of 1984, the Mother of God expressed the wish, through Jelena, that the parishioners gather once a week, when there are fewer pilgrims, to participate at Holy Mass to enable her to give them instructions for their spiritual life. The Franciscans decided that the day should be Thursday. Attracted by the motive of the National Eucharistic Congress, they had chosen the day of the Eucharist.

Since March 1, 1984, parishioners came in greater number to the evening Mass every Thursday. The sermon is addressed directly to them. Since then, Our Lady has regularly given (every Thursday) her messages to the parishioners through the seer Maria Pavlovic. She gave these messages regularly, concluding on January 8, 1987. Since then, she gives these messages on the 25th of the month.

These messages of Our Lady are primarily directed to the parishioners of the Medjugorje parish. Our Lady says that she has selected this parish in a special way and that God has special plans with this parish. Thus, she wishes to lead and truly shield this parish with love; she wishes that all parishioners be truly converted. These messages are actually incentives to the parish in liturgical intervals of time, so they will live their conversion and completely give themselves to her. Our Lady wishes to educate the parishioners through her messages and prepare them so that they will be able to realize the plans of God.

We still do not know what these plans of God and Our Lady are. For now, it is evident (and Our Lady said it specifically), the parishioners are to live her messages and transfer them to the pilgrims who come in such large numbers to Medjugorje, in order to find the origin of conversion there.

From the very beginning, it was clear that her messages are not limited to the parish of Medjugorje but directed to all people of good will who are ready to accept them and live them. And the faithful throughout the world, seed of Mary, accepted the messages of Our Lady with joy and enthusiasm. Her messages are immediately translated to other languages. They are accepted not only by the pilgrims who are there and who spread them farther, but they are transmitted by mail and telephone.

The numerous prayer groups in European countries and on other continents are very active in spreading the messages of Our Lady. Various publications and magazines print these messages. Some are created with the specific purpose of reporting about Medjugorje and printing articles about the messages and their explanations. The messages have also been published in separate booklets. There are many books that specifically deal with the messages of Our Lady. They are spread by radio as well. In some countries, it is possible to dial a telephone number and hear the latest message of Our Lady.

Innumerable souls find in Our Lady's messages an understanding and incentive for their spiritual life and growth in faith, and moving toward the realization of the will of God. We can say with certainty that the very acceptance of Mary's messages gives proof of the inner strength and power that God distributes here, and of the action of the Holy Spirit through these messages. At first glance, they are simple, so simple we could easily not grasp them and their profound meaning. But if we read them or listen to them attentively, if we think about them, if we contemplate over them and if we try to put them into practice, we discover their breadth and depth, all the wealth of their content and the strength of the graces that accompany them. We discover them to be a master-piece of pedagogy of Our Lady. Through them then, Our Lady has little by little introduced the parish of Medjugorje, and the rest of us who have tried to accept the messages, into a spiritual life and a life of prayer. She taught us how to live our conversion, and how to advance toward the final goal of living with God and in God, of the plan that God has with all of us and with each one of us.

Fr. Slavko Barbaric condenses this as follows: "In one of her messages, Our Lady said herself that she wishes us to hear her messages with the heart. This is the condition for them to become beneficial to us due to their simplicity. Motherly words are always simple and similar to each other, but full of love and that makes them beautiful. Thus, even before we read the messages and try to apply them in our lives, they create an atmosphere of confidence and love because the Mother speaks and wishes to lead. If we approach these short messages in this way, we will find in them all the depth and breadth of the love of God which is revealed through Mary. We will also discover the pedagogy, the upbringing that God gives us these days through Mary." (*Messages of Our Lady—Medjugorje, Sveta Bastina*, Duvno, 1987, pages 3-4.)

It is not practical to list all of the messages of Our Lady here. We are, therefore, selecting a small selection from the abundance that Our Lady gave us in her love. We should often read these messages, think about them and try to put them to work, "to live them," as Our Lady says. Many who have tried to accomplish this, experienced a special help and protection from Our Lady.

Dear children I have chosen this parish in a special way and I wish to lead it. I am guarding it with love and I wish everyone to be mine. Thank you for your response this evening. It is my wish that you always be here in greater numbers with me and my Son. Every Thursday, I will give you a special message. (March 1, 1984)

Dear children! Start converting yourselves here in this parish. This is my second wish. In that way all those who come here will likewise be able to convert. (March 8, 1984)

Adore continually the Blessed Sacrament. I am always present when the faithful are in adoration. Special graces are then being received. (March 15, 1984)

This evening I ask you especially to honor the Heart of my Son Jesus. Offer amends for the wounds caused to the Heart of my Son. That Heart was hurt by all kinds of sins. (April 5, 1984)

Today I ask you to stop slandering and to pray for the unity of the parish, because both my Son and I have a special plan for this parish. (April 12, 1984)

On August 14, 1984, the seer Ivan prayed at home. He then began to get ready to go to the church for the evening Mass. Our Lady suddenly and unexpectedly appeared to him. His surprise was so great that he was still confused when he came to the church. For him it was a big surprise because for a long time he experienced the apparitions only in the church. Our Lady told him to take to the world this message: *I would like that the world pray with me these days. And as much as possible! To fast strictly on Wednesday and Friday; to pray every day at least the Rosary; the Joyful, Sorrowful, and Glorious mysteries...* Our Lady also requested we accept this message with a strong will. She asked this especially of the parishioners and the faithful from the neighborhood.

On October 21, 1984, Our Lady requested that the Bible be in every house, in a visible place, and handy so that the Scriptures could be read every day.

"Prayer is the foundation and the first condition for any spiritual progress. Therefore, Our Lady leads us first into prayer, teaches us how to pray with our hearts. In her messages she talks the most often about prayer. According to the words of Our Lady, prayer does not consist of spending set time in prayer, longer or shorter, but that the prayer must envelope and saturate the whole day, every event, and every happening in our everyday life. Our Lady teaches us that prayer is the most important work, that we need prayer most, that we can and must attain everything by prayer. But she primarily wishes that we pray with our hearts, that prayer does not become an outside addition to life, but a necessity and reflection of life." (Fr. Ivan Dugandzic, *The Messages of Our Lady—Medjugorje*, page 89.)

The cross was in God's plan when you erected it. Especially during the present days; go on the hill and pray in front of the cross. I need your prayers. (August 23, 1984)

I wish to tell you today that you make me happy with your prayers at times, but there are many in the parish who do not pray, and my heart is sad. Therefore, pray so that I could take all your sacrifices and prayers to the Lord. (October 4, 1984)

You are not aware of the messages that God is sending through me. He is granting you great gifts and you do not understand. Pray that the Holy Spirit may enlighten you. If you knew how many graces God extends to you, you would pray without ceasing. (November 8, 1984)

During these days, Satan is in a special way evident in this parish. Pray that God's plan will be accomplished and that every action of Satan turns out to be for the honor of God. I have stayed here this long in order to help you in temptations. (February 7, 1985)

Message to priests: *I invite you to call everybody to pray the Rosary. With the Rosary you will conquer all troubles which Satan now wishes to make for the Catholic Church. Pray the Rosary! Devote your time to the Rosary!* (June 25, 1985)

I am calling you again to pray with your heart. If you pray with your heart, the ice in your brothers will melt and all the obstacles will disappear. Conversion will be easy for the ones who wish to accept it. This is a gift which you must get for your neighbor with your prayer. (January 23, 1986)

You are occupied with material things, but in material things you lose everything that God wishes to give you. I invite you to pray for the gifts of the Holy Spirit that you need to be able to testify to my presence here, and everything I am giving you. Leave it to me to lead you completely. Do not be occupied by material things. (April 17, 1986)

I call you today to start praying the Rosary with a live faith. In that way, I will be able to help you. You wish to receive graces but you do not advance. I invite you to pray the Rosary and that the Rosary become an obligation you will perform with joy. Then you will realize why I am with you for such a long time. I wish to teach you how to pray. (June 12, 1986)

Today, I call you all to prayer. Without prayer, you cannot feel God, nor me, nor the graces I am giving you. Therefore, I call you to always make prayer the beginning and the end of the day. I wish to lead you from day to day more into prayer, but you cannot grow if you do not want to. I invite you to put prayer in the first place. (July 3, 1986)

I wish today to call you to pray from day to day for the souls in Purgatory. Every soul needs prayer and grace to come to God and to God's love. And with such prayer, you will gain new intercessors who will help you in your life to be able to realize that all earthly things are not important to you, and that only Heaven is that what you should yearn for. Thus, pray without ceasing to help yourself and others, too, to which the prayers will bring joy. (November 6, 1986)

Today, too, I call you to prepare your hearts for the days when the Lord especially wishes to cleanse you from all the sins of your past. You cannot do it by yourself. Therefore, I am here to help you. Pray! This is the only way for you to be able to recognize all the evil that is in you and offer it to God, so that the Lord will completely clean your hearts. Thus, pray constantly and prepare your hearts in penance and fasting. (December 4, 1986)

Today again. I want to invite you from today on, to start to live a new life. I want you to comprehend that God has chosen each one of you in order to use you for the great plan of salvation for mankind. You cannot comprehend how great your role is in God's plan. Therefore, pray, that through prayer you may understand God's plan for you. I am with you so that you can realize it completely. (January 25, 1987)

Our Lady often calls attention in her messages to the danger that is threatening us from Satan. She calls for fasting and sacrifices. She often thanks us for everything we do for her. She calls us to read the Holy Scriptures and to go to Confession. And through all these messages, she slowly but surely leads us to a final goal which she openly requested several times and that is: that we become saints, that we live sanctity. Here are more messages about it:

I call you today to start fasting from your heart. There are many people who are fasting, but they fast because everyone else is fasting. This has become a habit that no one wants to break. I beg for the parish to fast as a thanksgiving to God that He is allowing me to remain for such a long time in this parish. Fast and pray with your heart! (September 20, 1984)

I thank you for all your prayers. Thank you for all your sacrifices. I wish to tell you that you should renew the messages I am giving you. Particularly, live by fasting, because with the fasting you will give me pleasure and you will help that the entire plan of God here in Medjugorje be accomplished. (September 26, 1985)

I call you today again, to prayer and fasting. You know that with your help, I can do anything and force Satan not to tempt people to do evil, and to leave this place. Satan lurks on each individual. He particularly wishes to bring confusion in everyday things, in each of you. Therefore I invite you that your day be only prayer and a complete surrender to God. (September 4, 1986)

I thank you for the love you show me. You know that I love you immensely and that I pray every day to Our Lord to help you realize the love that I am giving you. Therefore, pray, pray, pray! (August 21, 1986)

I invite you today to read the Bible every day in your homes, and the Bible should be in a visible place to always remind you to read it and to pray. (October 18, 1984)

Today I invite you to holiness. You cannot live without holiness. Therefore, you must overcome all sin with love. Overcome every difficulty you meet with love. I beg you to live love within yourself. (July 10, 1986)

Today also, I am calling you to pray with your whole heart and to change your life day by day. Especially, I am calling you that with your prayers and sacrifices, you start a life of holiness, because I wish that each one of you who is at this origin of grace, comes to Paradise with a special gift that he will offer to me. This gift is holiness. Therefore, pray from day to day, change your life to become holy. I will be forever close to you. (November 13, 1986)

I wish to invite all of you today that in the New Year, you live the messages I am giving you. You know that I stayed this long because of you, to teach you how to grow on the way to holiness. Therefore, pray constantly and live the messages I am giving you because I am doing it with a great love for God and for you. (January 1, 1987)

I call you today also, that each one of you decide to live the messages. God has allowed that in this year, which the Church has dedicated to me, I can speak and urge you to holiness. Beg from God the graces that He is giving you through me. I am ready to ask God for everything you request, to make your holiness complete. Therefore, do not forget to ask, because God has allowed me to obtain graces for you. (August 25, 1987)

I wish to call all of you today, that each one of you decides for Paradise. The way is hard for those who do not decide for God. Decide and believe that God offers Himself to you completely. You are invited and you must answer the call of the Father who calls you through me. Pray, because in prayer each one of you will be able to achieve complete love. I bless you and wish to help you so that each one of you will be under my motherly mantle. (October 25, 1987)

Today I call you again, that each one of you decide to give everything completely to me. Only in this way will I be able to offer each one of you to God. You know that I love you very much and that I wish to have each one of you for myself, but God has given everyone freedom that I respect—with love— and bow in my humility to your freedom. I wish that you would help, that everything that God has planned in this parish materializes. If you do not pray, you will not be able to discover my love, nor the plans that God has with this parish, and with each of you, individually. Pray that Satan does not attract you with his pride and deceptive strength. I am with you and I wish that you believe that I love you. (November 25, 1987)

I am calling you to abandon yourselves completely to God. Pray that Satan does not swing you about like a branch in the wind. Be strong in God. I wish that through you the entire world gets to know the God of joy. Be witnesses of the joy of God with your lives. Do not be anxious or worried. God will help you and show you the way. I wish that with my love, you love all, both the good and the evil. Only in this way, love will reign over the world. Dear children, you are mine. I love you and I wish that you would surrender yourselves to me so that I can lead you to God. Pray continually so that Satan cannot take advantage of you. Pray to recognize that you are mine. I am blessing you with a blessing of joy. (May 25, 1988)

"Today I am calling you to a love that is loyal and pleasing to God. Little children, love accepts everything, everything that is hard and bitter for the sake of Jesus who is love. Therefor, pray to God that He come to your aid, but not according to your desires, but in accordance with His love. Abandon yourselves to God so that He can heal you, console you, and forgive you of everything in you that stands as a barrier on the way of love. In this way, God will be able to form your life, and you will grow in love. Glorify God, little children, with psalms of love, so that God's love will be able to grow from day to day to its fullness." (June 25, 1988)

"I am asking you from today to accept the way of holiness. I love you, and therefore I want you to be holy. I do not wish that Satan distract you from this way. Pray and accept everything offered you by God that is bitter on this way. But in the same way, whoever begins to follow Him, God reveals all the sweetness, and he will gladly respond to each and every one of His calls. Do not consider the importance of trivial things! Yearn for Heaven!" (July 25, 1988)

A SUDDEN CONVERSION

From the pastor of Gornja Stubica:

His parishioner, Milan Brezak, for a long time was known as a nonbeliever. He publicly acted as such, and lived as such, in everything. Neither he, nor anyone from his house went to church, and he raised his children in the same way. At the end of 1982, he got cancer, without any hope of recovery. Many faithful tried to convince him to go to Confession, but he stubbornly rejected it. Quite a number of faithful from the parish have made the pilgrimage to Medjugorje. These pilgrims prayed for him in particular, in Medjugorje, and at home. On one occasion, the visionaries recommended him specially to Our Lady. He himself told what happened and the people in his house testify that it is true.

On Thursday, March 3, 1983, after he had lunch in bed, his wife took the dishes to the kitchen. It was around three o'clock in the afternoon. He turned to the other side of the bed. On the wall, he noticed the figure of Our Lady, only the upper half of the body. He looked at it about one minute. She looked at him but did not say anything—she was only smiling. He was completely conscious, awake and scared. He stared at her because he never saw such unusual beauty. After, he cried all day, but did not say anything to anyone.

The next day, he told his wife and some others what he saw. He asked for Confession. The pastor came, heard his confession and gave him Holy Communion. Since then he often received Communion. He said that if God would give him back his health, he would never miss the Mass on Sunday.

Ten days after his vision, some friends came to visit him. The sick man told them consciously, in detail, about his illness and the operation he had, and then especially about what he saw and experienced. He showed on the wall the circle in which he saw the figure of Our Lady. He stated that nobody in the world could make him stop talking about what he saw. When it was most difficult for him, he asked the people in the house to pray together with him, day and night. After he had read a book about Medjugorje, he asked that his son go there with a group of pilgrims. So, the son went to Medjugorje, and upon returning, he stated that he saw an unusual sign on the cross at the top of the hill. Others in the group saw it too. The conversion of the sick man was quickly made known to many and many came to see him. He talked to everyone about conversion, about God and Our Lady. He died three months later, at the beginning of June 1983, completely calm and trusting in God's will.

Our Lady said that she would come to any house if it were necessary. And this case shows that she seriously meant what she said.

A TESTIMONY ABOUT MEDJUGORJE

Professor von Lobkowitz, President of the University of Eichstatt, is certainly one of the greatest personalities of the Catholic laymen movement at the present time. At the invitation of Cardinal Hoffner, he attended a conference of deacons in Koln and gave a very interesting talk about the consequences of the Vatican Council II. Among other things, he talked about Medjugorje. (The entire lecture has been printed in "Deutsche Tagespost," the issue of 19/20, November, 1985.) In part, he said:

"In all corners and parts of the world, something new has suddenly appeared, at first among young people. That is now spreading quickly, as if somebody has thrown many pebbles in the muddy, deceivingly smooth swamp of the present age. In the first place, the unusual phenomena is a small village, Medjugorje, in Yugoslavia, where six children, since June 24, 1981, report that the Mother of God appears to them virtually daily for close to four years. It is not my duty to bring judgment about the truth of these events, even in the light of Lourdes and Fatima, though I am not afraid to openly state that, after all that I have seen, read, and learned, I am convinced that there, in the middle of a Marxist state, the Mother of God actually appears. For me there remains only the theoretical question of the comprehension of what it actually means. Why do I mention these phenomena here, and why right in the beginning?

"A few years ago, it was unthinkable to imagine such a power of radiation and action as is now coming from Medjugorje. Almost daily, people (mostly young), travel by trains, cars, and crowded buses for hundreds of miles, just to be there. They travel, not out of curiosity, but to pray, to convert, to fast at least once a week on bread and water. And, that is not all. They come back and start a completely new life. A month later, they travel again to Medjugorje.

"There are no politics, no beating on a guitar, no usual pilgrimage tumult, but five to eight hours in the church, up to five rosaries a day, and when they return, at least one rosary a week, often daily. The same young people, who a few months ago thought of everything except prayer, now regularly go to Confession and participate in Holy Mass, almost daily. They urge others of their own age to travel there, too. Which parish in the world could report that they annually distributed hundreds of thousands of Communions and that all communicants went to confession before that? That during only one novena in the summer 1984, almost 60,000 received Holy Communion? That during 42 months, over four million pilgrims visited a large church in a small village of only seven hundred inhabitants, out in order to pray there; and not only Catholics, but Orthodox, Protestants, Baptists, and even Moslems?! Even if these data are exaggerated—and nothing indicates that they are—and if I withhold my final judgment about the verity of the apparitions, the phenomenon in Medjugorje testifies about the recent unthinkable yearning, (but also readiness) of specifically these young people to break through the hedonistic desperation of the present time, into a direction of radical conversion, new spirituality, and an integral Christian way of life."

OUR LADY HERSELF FINDS COWORKERS

The American, Wayne Weible, a columnist from Myrtle Beach, South Carolina, speaks about an event that completely changed his life:

"As a Lutheran Protestant I knew nothing about the Virgin

Mary. I first heard about Medjugorje in a Sunday School Class I was teaching at a Lutheran church. Toward the end of the class, someone mentioned what was happening in Yugoslavia in this little village. As a publisher of four weekly community newspapers and a columnist, I was curious to find out more.

After the class, I asked the person who had mentioned it where she had heard about it. She directed me to a mutual friend who had a book and a video-tape on the background of the alledged appearances. Several nights later my wife and I settled down to watch the video tape.

What happened during the viewing of that video changed my life completely. I suddenly 'felt' a strong message within myself. In essence it said, 'You are my son, and you are to do my Son's work. Write about the events in Medjugorje. Afterwards, you will no longer be in this work (newspapers), for your life will be devoted to the spreading of the message.'

There was no doubt in my heart about the source of the message. It was from Mary, the Blessed Virgin. I just kept wondering, why me? I knew so little and felt totally unworthy.

In December (1985), I began a series of four columns on the apparitions. In March 1986, our newspaper business was sold. Just as predicted in the message, my work is now dedicated to spreading the message of Medjugorje.

The above story is merely a reflection of hundreds of similar stories duplicated around the world. New organizations (groups and individuals), new apostolates and ministries have sprung up, all dedicated to spreading the messages from the Mother of God at Medjugorje. Most of these are charitable organizations that do not follow "for profit" incentives. They produce and distribute books, films and newsletters. They organize programs, pilgrimages, and give talks.

The western world, with its great resources and freedom, seems to have leapt to the forefront in this noble work. England, Ireland, Italy, France, and especially the United States, now provide many ministries dedicated to this effort.

"HE SHOULD PERSIST IN PRAYER AND FAST!"

A young family I knew, found itself in a difficult, hopeless situation. The problem could not be solved by human criteria. Through Vicka, I recommended that family to Our Lady in the spring of 1982. She answered: "Everything will be all right."

But nothing was better; to the contrary, it was even worse. After half a year I once again met the father of that family in Medjugorje. Through Maria, we directed our petition again to Our Lady: "Our Lady, you have promised that everything will be going well, but things are not good, they're even worse!" Our Lady's response was: *I have not forgotten my promise. He should persist in prayer and fasting.*

The young father suffered very much. Several times he was tempted to give up. I consoled him and encouraged him: "I still believe in the promise of Our Lady!" He persevered for almost three full years. And then the problem was solved. And that trial was somehow for their good. It brought a great progress in faith, conversion and depth of life, through faith in God.

PART FOUR

MOTHER AND HEALER

HEALINGS

A sign that apparitions are true is the manifestation of the grace of God in souls. This is evident through conversions and the renewal of the entire relgious life. In Medjugorje, indeed there is no lack of that. But Medjugorje also has visible signs of healings which are credited to the intercession of Our Lady.

By the end of August 1981, in the parish office in Medjugorje, there were over 100 such cases. And as time passed, more such cases were reported. Not all cases are great miracles, but most of them show evidence of God's help given by the intercession of Our Lady to her children who were in trouble. Many healings did not happen suddenly but gradually, after a period of time. For most, there is no medical documentation and it may never be possible to obtain it. Most certainly, there are a great number of healings that for some reason are not registered anywhere, but remain unknown, and the persons who received these graces thank Our Lady in the privacy of their hearts.

There are, however, great healings for which there is sizable medical documentation. It is not possible to enumerate all cases. I am mentioning here only a few healings that happened by the intercession of Our Lady in Medjugorje.

JOZO VASILJ

Old Jozo Vasilj was the first in Medjugorje who was healed by the intercession of Our Lady. In the 1970's, he became paralyzed on the left side of his body. He was completely blind in his left eye. He developed open wounds on his paralyzed left arm that would not heal. By the early 1980's, he became blind in his right eye. He was helpless and had to be lead everywhere.

When he heard about the apparitions on Podbrdo, he said: "I will tell you whether or not it is Our Lady!" He asked a neighbor to bring him a little soil and weeds with thorns from the place of apparitions. The neighbor was reluctant, but he went anyway and brought it to the old man. Jozo mixed the soil and weeds with water in a container and washed his face with that muddy water, praying the Creed. He rinsed himself with clean water, dried himself with a towel, and said to his wife:

"My old one, I see you!"

"Don't be crazy, how could you see me when you have been completely blind for four years!"

"Aren't you ashamed, you are an old woman and you walk around without stockings?" Then she believed. Of course, the joy was indescribable.

Then, with the same muddy water Jozo washed his left arm, from the shoulder to the fingertips, and wrapped it in a towel. The next morning, there was no trace of wounds. His pastor testified that all this was true.

Everybody says that Jozo was always very pious. After the healing, he was often unable to sleep and so he prayed. He prayed the rosary and the litany. "During my whole life, I will not be able to thank dear God enough."

Two years later, Jozo died in his 87th year of age.

THE ORTHODOX CHILD

In Medjugorje sometime during 1981, a sick child of an Orthodox gypsy family was healed. One priest was surprised that that was possible. The seer Maria said after that: "It was very troublesome for me to hear that. If I heard it from somebody else, I could take it! But it bothers me that a priest should say that! I mentioned it to Our Lady and she said:

"Tell that priest and everyone else, that you have divided

*yourselves on the earth. Moslems, Orthodox and Catholics
are all my children.''*

DIANA BASILE IS GRATEFUL FOR THE HEALING

Diana Basile from Milan, Italy, married, and a mother of
three children, was born on October 25, 1940, and had been
taken ill by multiple sclerosis in the year 1972. That was the
diagnosis of the University Clinic in Milan. She was completely blind in the right eye; she had impediments in moving
that caused the paralysis of her upper and lower extremities
(arms and legs). She was incontinent and that caused a skin
irritation. She came to Medjugorje in a wheelchair and was
healed on May 23, 1984.

She brought 121 testimonies from physicians about her illness. She has reports of many physicians about her cure. Among
others, four Italian physicians testified: "The testing of vision
of the right eye that was blind, shows 100% vision now, while
the healthy eye has a vision of only 90%." On May 23, 1986,
Diana came again to Medjugorje and after the evening Mass,
said the following prayer of thanksgiving:

"I thank the Mother of God from all my heart. She hears
us. She loves us and wishes to have us around her. Let us
give her our hearts as a gift. Queen of Peace, pray for us!"

LILIANA SMREKAR

Liliana Smrekar from Udine, Italy, a 54 year old teacher,
had an accident in 1983 when she was leaving the school.
Two cars collided and knocked her down, hurting her left
knee. She was taken to the hospital where she had surgery.
Her leg was in a cast for 60 days, but the knee did not return
to the proper position. Then she had another operation which
made things worse. In February 1985, she had a very complicated operation by a famous French surgeon, after which, she
could move only on crutches. Her knee was heavily damaged

in the accident and even more so by the operations. It was held together by pins and screws. The leg could not support the weight of her body and she had to use crutches for even the smallest motion. The illness and loneliness was devastating, and she was on the verge of a nervous breakdown.

In January 1985, when she was waiting for the examination of the surgeon before the third operation, she looked through the magazines that she found in the waiting room. There were several issues of the review *Gente,* and in one, she found an article about Medjugorje. She read it with interest and immediately had the wish to go there. She could not travel by bus because of her condition, but had the opportunity to go by pickup truck with only a few pilgrims. They started on Friday, June 7, 1985. She was very nervous. She states:

"I left with a thousand difficulties. I left my old sick mother home. It is not true that I had wanted a cure at any price. I prayed to Our Lady in my own way. We stayed in Medjugorje two days, which were terrible for me. It seemed that everything happened to me. I experienced more pain than usual in my knee. I moved with more difficulty on the crutches. I was overcome by anxiety, and had the feeling that I would suffocate, especially when I tried to enter the church to pray. Unexplainable! I could not breathe. I did not have any strength; I perspired. I was in a rage! I had to leave! It was as if somebody was in me, who did not want me to go to pray to Our Lady."

On Saturday afternoon they persuaded her to go to Confession. They brought her to a Capuchin father who spoke Italian. The Capuchin father suggested that she take oil and water and give them to one of the visionaries who would present them to Our Lady for blessing during the apparition. After Confession she was restless and in tears. Somebody took the water and oil to Vicka, and asked her to present it to Our Lady to bless them. In the evening, before she went to bed, Liliana greased her painful knee with the blessed oil, but she did not feel better. Because of the great pain, she could not sleep all night.

On Sunday, June 9, 1985, when she wanted to enter the church, she almost fainted. She had to go back out. In the evening, they took her to Vicka, where she attended the apparition in her home. When Vicka fell on her knees, Liliana jerked. Her face suddenly brightened and her eyes were filled with tears from excitement. After the apparition, they took her with the pickup truck to the parking lot and from there they started to walk to the church. Holy Mass had already begun.

Liliana then felt that she could stand and walk without crutches. She was very excited, but did not dare to throw away the crutches. To convince herself that it was not a hallucination, she constantly put weight on the left, painful leg. She walked carrying the crutches in her hands, ready to use them again. She went to Communion without crutches.

"I made my first steps with fear, but I felt great. I passed through the whole nave, among many people, progressing slowly. I burst into tears, but these were tears of joy and thanksgiving. My knee was still painful, but I could walk. It is up to the physicians to explain that mysterious phenomenon." (According to the article written by the newspaperman Renzo Allegri in the review *Gente* from July 5, 1985).

AGNES HEUPEL

Agnes Heupel from Munster, Westfalen, Germany, born January 29, 1951, was a medical nurse, the fourth and only living child of her parents. Her father died in 1977. She married a Catholic, in church, October 5, 1973. She became hurt when she supported a heavy patient. She felt some cracking in her spine, accompanied with severe pain, and that was the beginning of a suffering that lasted 12 years.

The lower part of her spine was heavily damaged. Medication did not help. She had two operations, 1975 and 1976. After the second operation, her diagnosis was: "Partial paralysis with disturbances of the bladder and the colon, all incurable."

In addition, she incurred new troubles; an inflammation of the nerve muscles on her face and a tumor on her lungs. The physicians could not do anything for her but to prescribe the strongest pain killer medicines. These medicines, in turn, caused disturbances in her memory, so that she had to walk around with a notebook, because she had to make notes of everything she had to do—she could not remember anything.

She had no feeling in her legs. She moved either on crutches on in a wheelchair, She drove a car adjusted for invalids. She always had to keep pills handy for the pain, and to take them when she needed them.

Then, her marriage broke down. Her husband did not take care of her when she was sick. He left her and asked for a divorce after one year separation. Her husband was not a believer, and living with him, she had neglected her prayers. If the marriage lasted longer, she would have probably completely lost her faith. She returned to her parents home to live with her mother.

Three years before her healing, she saw in a dream, a white church that was completely unknown to her. Several months later, someone gave her a book about Medjugorje. Then she recognized the church she had seen in her dream. On March 2 and 3, 1986, she met Fr. Slavko Barbaric who gave a lecture about Medjugorje. He prayed over her and talked with her. She decided she would go to Medjugorje, alone, by car, without a companion, and without the wheelchair.

Since childhood, she honored Our Lady, but, as like many others, nothing special. The rosary was boring to her. But in her suffering she found, little by little, the way to God. She started to pray.

On May 1, 1986, she arrived in Medjugorje after four days of traveling a distance of 2,000 kilometers. She began her journey with two crutches, but she always left one in the car. In Medjugorje she made friends with some pilgrims, regularly attended the Mass, and started to pray much more.

On the morning of May 12th, Fr. Slavko told her: "This evening you can come to the apparition."

First she gave a sigh of relief, "Thank God!" Then, she walked around the church all day long, "like a chased dog," as she herself says. She could not find peace anywhere; she was nervous. In the church, she did not find peace either. Then, a young American came to her rescue. In the yard of the parish house, they prayed the rosary together. She was present at the apparition in a room of the rectory.

During the apparition her feeling of confusion and nervousness immediately disappeared. Suddenly she was calm. "I felt that the Mother of God was there and sensed the origin of peace at the point where all the eyes of the seers were directed."

That day, Ivan and Maria were present at the apparition. Agnes lowered herself from the bed on which she was sitting, to her knees. She attempted to recommend to Our Lady all who were present. At that moment, she did not pray for herself at all. She lost the sense of time. In her face something started to "burn." She felt a warm stream from her face downward. It spread through her whole body. She says that she could not describe it.

After the apparition she started toward the door with the others. There stood Fr. Slavko—"You forgot something." Agnes did not understand. "There is your crutch, take it." She took the crutch, but did not know what to do with it. She left the crutch in the car and went to the church. She pushed toward the front through masses of people. Some acquaintances in the front benches asked her: "Where is your crutch?"

"What do I need the crutch for?" And only then she realized what actually happened to her.

She came to Medjugorje as a wreck of a human being, and she returned completely cured, and spiritually and mentally completely renewed.

After that she visited Medjugorje several times and always stayed a long time. She brought with her all the medical documentation about her illness and her cure. (According to Norbert Ortmanns: *Steh auf and geh - Kirche Leben*—["Stand up and go - Church Life"], publication of the diocese of Munster, No. 49, December 12, 1986 and *Krsni Zavicaj*, No. 19, 1986, pages 276-287).

ALCOHOL AND DRUG ABUSERS

In Medjugorje, many alcoholics and drug abusers were healed. Often there could be found entire groups of abusers who tried to find, and who actually did find, a cure to their trouble. A cured alcoholic, a middle-aged man, tells the following:

"I drank daily at least half a liter of hard liquor. In spite of many attempts, I could not break the habit. I started to pray and fast. And members of my family prayed. And then suddenly, I did not need any more of those promises that I did not keep anyway. I simply did not have the need for alcohol anymore." His gray-haired mother listened and added with a happy smile, "I, too, my son, did much praying and fasting for you!"

RITA MARY KLAUS

On July 20th, 1987, I met an American, Mrs. Rita Mary Klaus, in Medjugorje. She was from Evans City, Pennsylvania, United States of America. She was probably close to 50 years old, and was there with her husband and three children. She was strong and robust in stature and evidently full of life and health. She told me her story:

"I suffered 26 years from the consequences of multiple sclerosis. The last seven years were especially difficult. My illness became more difficult because of a complete paralysis of legs and deformation of both knees. I had several operations on my right leg. The physicians wanted to ease the shrinking of the muscles. They tried to set the kneecap into the proper position. I had difficulty with emptying my bladder, and was incontinent. I suffered from infections and severe hindrances in my vision. I could hardly distinguish the objects around me. My right hand was shaking so that I could hardly write a few lines. My handwriting was impossible.

"With the aid of crutches, I could move around a little in our home, but I spent most of my time in the wheelchair. With generous help from my husband, I cooked, did the laundry and cleaned. Our three daughters, though still young (7, 10 and 12 years old) learned how to help me. With the help of a good friend, and fellow teachers, it was made possible for me to continue teaching at our parish school of St. Gregory in Zelienople."

I wanted to know how was she cured. She said:

"It was on a Wednesday, June 18, 1986. In the evening, after the daily work was finished, I prayed the usual daily rosary. I suddenly had the idea to pray to Jesus for my health, by the intercession of Our Lady in Medjugorje. I was never before in Medjugorje. Recently, I read in some Catholic publications about the apparitions there, and I just finished reading the book "Is the Virgin Mary Appearing in Medjugorje?" by René Laurentin. That book gave me the incentive to fast several days a week. I never prayed before for my cure, but only to be able to do what is God's will, well and with joy.

"When I prayed to Our Lady to intercede for me that I receive the grace of cure, I felt a wave of electricity through my entire body. At that moment, I felt peace as never before. After that I felt very tired and fell asleep.

"The next morning I drove to La Roche College where I attended a short course in Bible studies. Suddenly, during the lecture, I realized that I could again feel my legs, and I started to move my toes which I was not able to do for over ten years. I remember practically nothing from the lecture. I just sat there and moved my toes.

"Because of the large deformities on my knees, I had steel braces on each side of my legs, held together by a ring around the knees and ankles. When I came home, I wanted to take these supports off because it was hot. When I looked at my legs, I noticed that the deformities were gone. The legs were straightened. I was overcome with so much joy that I shouted and thanked God and Mary.

"I removed the supports from my legs, took my crutches and started to climb the steps to the second floor. I said to myself: 'If I am cured, I will be able to climb the steps.'

"And—I succeeded! Then, I ran through the whole house. I had to share my happiness with someone. Since my husband went with the children to a farm to pick strawberries, I called our priest. In the excitement, I dialed my own telephone number. Finally I got him, but it seemed that he did not believe me. Then I called my best friend, Marianne Nock, who lives on the same street. I was crying so much, from joy, that she thought something terrible had happened. She came immediately. We laughed and cried together.

"Then we started for the farm to surprise my husband and my children. Since the pastor's house was on our way, we stopped and showed him what happened. Without any help, I knelt down and asked for his blessing.

"When we arrived at the farm, my family was already on their way home. So, we returned, too. At home I showed my husband and the children. When we calmed down a little, my husband called Dr. Angelo Vierra in the Center for Rehabilitation Harmaville, in Pittsburgh.

Dr. Vierra could not believe it. He saw me exactly a month ago during my last examination, which I had every three months. At that time he could not observe any change in my condition, except that I lost weight, probably from fasting. Dr. Vierra wanted to see me as soon as possible, but because of the weekend, we made an appointment for Monday, June 23, at 12 o'clock.

"The result of the examination was clear. There was no trace of multiple sclerosis. All reflexes were normal, the sense of equilibrium and the strength of muscles were normal, the shaking disappeared.

"Dr. Vierra simply could not believe it. He had never seen anything like that. All signs of deformity had disappeared, and there was no longer any paralysis. He said that I am now like a newly-born person, and I should start a new life. 'Go home, go to church, and thank God!' "

The same physician issued a written testimony about the cure, and other physicians confirmed it. In his document it says:

"The patient does not need any means of help. Both legs returned to their full strength. The sense of equilibrium and reaction of senses are good. She hopped on one leg, with her eyes closed, and it was no problem. The test of nerves on the legs under the knees, and on foot soles, show regular findings.

In the same way, the reflexes on the tendons showed that they are symmetrical and normal. As a whole, the patient has experienced an incomprehensible cure."

I asked Mrs. Klaus how she felt now. "Excellent!" I saw the photographs of her knees as they were before the healing. And now, I could see with my own eyes that there are no traces of any growth or deformities.

She continued her story: "I often testify about my miraculous healing. Sometimes I talk to very large groups of people. I've talked already to many thousands in thanksgiving for what God has done to me through the intercession of Our Lady at Medjugorje. I give the talks not only in the United States, but also in Canada. In this way, many people hear about the messages from Medjugorje which bring peace and hope. I thank God daily, and His Blessed Mother, for the grace they have given me.

"During my lectures, many people convert and receive the Sacraments. This in itself is a miracle for me, and I thank God that he gives these graces through me.

"I would advise all who are seriously ill, that they seek God's will in their severe suffering. Everything comes from the hands of God—health and sickness. We should receive both with joy and peace. But we can do that only if we have completely surrendered to the will of God."

This healing was the reason that her three brothers and a sister returned to the Faith and the Church. Her five nephews and nieces, at the ages of 10 to 25 years, allowed themselves to be baptized and on Easter 1987, they received their first Holy Communion. Mrs. Klaus says: "We should give thanks for that to God, and to His Holy Mother!"

On July 25, 1987, on the feast of the apostle St. James, the patron saint of the parish of Medjugorje, Mrs. Rita Klaus testified in the church in Medjugorje about her cure, and in great love and thanksgiving, in the overcrowded church, sang the "Magnificat" ("My Soul Glorifies the Lord"), the song that the Mother of God, long ago, sang out in her gratefulness because of the conception of the Son of God. All present were deeply moved by this testimony that told them about the power of God and about the great love of Our Lady and the power of her intercession.

KARLO IVANKOVIC

Karlo Ivankovic is from Ljubuski, married, father of three children, and born on August 1, 1940. I visited him in his house on July 21, 1987. On this occasion he told me the following of his experience:

In the summer of 1983, he fell ill to virus jaundice—"hepatitus B." He was sick for three months. He was admitted to the hospital in Mostar on October 26, 1983. He did not eat anything for 25 days. His liver stopped functioning, and he lost 12 kilograms of weight. His whole body was of an intensive yellow color. At that time, he was not aware of anything around him. On Friday, November 18 the physicians said: "He will hold through only this night."

He was a good believer before, too. He fasted on Wednesdays and Fridays according to the wish of Our Lady. He often came to Medjugorje. During his illness, his family and many others prayed for him.

On that Friday, November 18, 1983, in the evening, suddenly an indescribable spiritual and bodily peace came over him, a peace he could not describe. Time and space did not exist for him. He heard a voice that cannot be exactly defined, whether it was a male or a female voice, or a human voice at all, a voice like a light ringing; but it was completely clear and understandable to him.

"My child, what are you afraid of? Open up, tell me what is bothering you."

His first thought was: This is the Lady of Medjugorje! "My Lady of Medjugorje, it seems to me that it is early for me to go away. I have a wife and three small children and a sick old mother. They still need me."

Then, he suddenly found himself in the church in Medjugorje. It was a concelebrated evening Mass, led by the pastor Fr. Tomislav Pervan, in green garments. (Later Karlo asked and found out that Fr. Tomislav Pervan actually led that evening Mass.) It was just at the end of the sermon. He remained until the Consecration. Then he found himself again at his old place in the hospital, in a state of perfect peace. The same voice also told him: "Child, do not be afraid, everything will be all right." Then he fell asleep, or perhaps it was all a dream.

In the morning, a doctor woke him up. He was in his room, on the bed. "Karlo, how do you feel?"

"Fantastic! I am hungry, give me something to eat!"

During the examination, the doctors found that he was now a healthy man. There was no trace of jaundice virus in his body. Since that time, Karlo lives a completely normal life, eats everything and works at his regular chores. There was never again any trace of jaundice for him.

To tell the truth, it should be stated that the physicians tried to give him, during the last days of his illness, a medication which is not usually given for jaundice. It is called Pronison. But if Karlo was healed by this medication, he would have had to keep a strict diet for the rest of his life, otherwise he would not be able to live and work normally. After the cure, the doctor only said: "In medicine things happen sometimes that cannot be explained."

And something else—for a long time, several years before that illness, Karlo had a strong migraine from which he suffered almost every day. No medications helped. Since the morning he was cured from the jaundice, the migraine also disappeared, and to this day, he has never had even the slightest headache.

Karlo says that during all his life, he will not be able to give enough thanks to God and Our Lady, for the grace that he has received.

PART FIVE

POSITION OF
THE CHURCH
AND CONCLUSION

COMMISSIONS FOR MEDJUGORJE

The bishop of Mostar, Msgr. Pavao Zanic, by his decree of January 11, 1982, established a commission of four members for an examination of the events in Medjugorje, in accordance with the rules of Church discipline and practice, and requested that Catholic media of public information in our country not report any more about these events. The request about not reporting does not have the power of strict binding, but our Catholic publications, in general, obeyed the request.[1]

In February 1984, Msgr. Zanic enlarged the commission to 14 members, 13 priests and one doctor of psychiatry. Later, another physician joined them.

"Crkva na Kamenu" (Church on the Rock), the organ of the diocese of Mostar, in issue No. 5/84, printed the conversation with Dr. Rudolf Brajcic, SJ, a member of the expanded commission, and the article was reprinted in the weekly "Glas Koncila" (Voice of the Council) in the issue No. 10, March 13, 1984. Among others, Father Brajcic says:

> "We would all be happy and pleased if in Medjugorje the apparitions of Our Lady were truly occurring. In addition, we are dealing with the problem here of bringing to judgment whether or not the finger of God is at work in Medjugorje, which in essence means to be the judge of God, to judge His works, which is not at all easy. Therefore, in our statement to the press we asked for help with prayers."

The expanded commission on Medjugorje met for the last time on May 2, 1986. After that, Msgr. Zanic handed over the whole case to the Vatican as requested. Urged by the Vatican, the Bishops' Conference of Yugoslavia took over the whole situation in their own hands. On January 29, 1987, a statement about it was made public. The statement was signed by Cardinal Franjo Kuharic, president of the Bishops' Conference of Yugoslavia, and Pavao Zanic, bishop of Mostar. The statement says:

> "The Bishops' Conference of Yugoslavia instituted a Commission with the purpose of continuing the examination of the events in Medjugorje. In awaiting the results of the work of this Commission and the judgment of the Church, shepherds, and the faithful should respect the stand of customary rationality in such situations. Therefore, it is not allowed to organize pilgrimages or other manifestations, with a supernatural character attributed to the events in Medjugorje. A devotion to Mary, which is legal and recommended by the Church, must be in accordance with the directives of the Magisterium, and, in particular, with the directives of the Apostolic incentive *Marialis Cultus* (Veneration of Mary, February 2, 1974)."

The publication "Marija" in the issue 6/87 carries the following note about that Commission: "The new Commission of the Bishops' Conference of Yugoslavia for the examination of the events in Medjugorje began to work on April 9. The work will not be open to the public nor will it issue statements for the public, and the result of the work will be submitted to the final judgment of the National Bishops' Conference."

Nothing was known about the number of the Commission members, who are the members, or where and when the Commission meets.

"Medjugorje—Gebesaktion," No. 5, 1987, published the conversation with the archbishop of Split, Msgr. Franic on December 5, 1986. In this conversation, Msgr. Franic says:

> "The Commission of the diocese of Mostar worked for several years, from 1982 to 1986. This was the

Bishop's Advisory Commission. A majority of the Commission members, as I heard, took a negative position, some were neutral, and some took a positive stance. The bishop of Mostar repeatedly expressed himself negatively toward Medjugorje. He stated, 'That we deal here with a fraud, a fraud of the Franciscans.'

"The Holy See did not approve the results of this Commission on the basis of other information received. The Holy See requested from the Bishops' Conference of Yugoslavia to form another Commission that would be responsible to the National Bishops Conference (and not to the local bishop, as was customary until now in such cases). By the aid of this new Commission, which is still being formed, the Bishops' Conference has also to examine other very voluminous documents from theologians and from other scientists.

"To the statement of the Bishops' Conference of Yugoslavia, I offer the following: "Official" pilgrimages to Medjugorje and similar places are not allowed. But all faithful, also every bishop and priest, has the right and *is* allowed to make a pilgrimage to any church, alone or in an organized group, and nobody can forbid it. About the events in Medjugorje, free discussions are possible; everybody is free to accept them or not. This is the opinion, publicly and repeatedly stated by the archbishop of Split and president of the Commission for Religious Teaching at the Bishops' Conference of Yugoslavia, Msgr. Franic."

There were no "official" pilgrimages to Medjugorje and nobody even attempted to undertake something like that. And if the faithful from so many countries and nations in the world, in so many numbers, come to a pilgrimage there and show so many evident fruits in their lives from these pilgrimages, it is a sign that they use the graces that God so generously provides there. Could or should that be forbidden to them?

A Swiss pastor who several times led pilgrimages to Medjugorje, said this:

"It is wrong to await the decision of a local bishop or of Rome to make a pilgrimage to Medjugorje. If everybody waited that long concerning Lourdes and Fatima, those pilgrimage places would have never been acknowledged. We would have missed the fruits of the apparitions and would not have the necessary witnesses." (*Sonntag, Olten,* No. 23 of June 23, 1987; *Marienerscheinungen in Medjugorje, Ende oder Wende?*) (Mary's Apparitions in Medjugorje, End or Turning Point?)

Concerning the caution that devotion to Mary must be in accordance with the directives of the Church Magisterium, I dare to remark:

The essence of the teaching of the Church about the devotion to Mary, as the Church preached and lived for centuries, is that Mary must lead to Jesus, to God, according to the principle—Through Mary to Jesus.

Whoever came to Medjugorje and observed the hapenings there, particularly in the church, and around the church, must have concluded the fact that the center of the entire devotion and services in the church, is Jesus Christ, Son of God and Redeemer of the world. It is Holy Mass and distribution of the Sacraments, in the services by words in the sermons, the adoration of the Most Holy Eucharist and the adoration of the Cross. In Medjugorje, this is expressed and stressed much more clearly than, for example, in Marija Bistrica, the Croatian national shrine, and it seems to me, more clearly and more obviously, than even Lourdes and Fatima.

I also feel that it is not proper that anyone claim the right to prohibit the religious press to report about Medjugorje. Every person and every believer has the right, according to the law of God and man, to be informed. The events in Medjugorje have taken such proportions, that practically no believer (and I would say, no human being), can remain indifferent toward them. Until the official Church states her judgment, everybody has a right to create an opinion for himself on the basis of common sense, and the principle of Christ's Gospel—*By their fruits you will know them.* (*Mt.* 7:16).

It is a fact that other nations, even outside Europe, are very well informed about the events in Medjugorje, and about the messages of Our Lady. Only we, who are here at the origin, know and are able to learn so little about everything.

CONCLUSION

I am aware of the fact that my report is not perfect. It has its shortcomings. First of all, it is not complete. But I can state that I have tried with the greatest care to truthfully present the events as much as was possible for me. If this book will help only one person to find Our Lady, and through her to return to God, I will consider my efforts not to be in vain, but, on the contrary they would be abundantly rewarding.

While working on this book, I had to intensively deal with the apparitions of Our Lady and her messages. As a result I can say that I was the one who had the greatest gain from this book and this work. How many perceptions and incentives I obtained for my personal spiritual and priestly life! Never before in my life did I find in spiritual literature, though I have read very much, something that could conjure up in my fancy and let me so intensely experience the love of Our Lady and God toward men, toward all of us.

Here, in the way Our Lady appears, in the words she speaks and the messages she sends, the motherly love of Our Lady reached my heart and my mind intimately and closely. I have experienced that love extraordinarily vividly, clearly and deeply in my consciousness and in my feelings. I believe that through eternity, I could not give enough thanks to God and to Our Lady for these graces and cognitions. Without them, my life, especially my spiritual life, would have been poor.

For me personally, these experiences are the strongest, the most certain, and the most trustworthy proof of the verity of the apparitions of Our Lady in Medjugorje. They are giving me strength—fully aware of my conviction—to testify for Our Lady.

I have experienced the love of God and Our Lady. I wish to transmit this experience to others, to everyone who is ready and willing to accept it. I wish and I pray to Our Lady to ask for everyone the grace to experience the same.

I hope this book will help as large a number of people, and my brothers, as possible, to find Our Lady and her love. May they, too, fall in love with Jesus Christ and His Mother, and I pray that Our Lady would then lead them to the eternal, endless, incomprehensible—but still so vivid, real and so close to us—love of God.

On July 21, 1987, I asked Jelena Vasilj to give me a message from Our Lady for this book. Without hesitation she transmitted to me these words of Our Lady:

If you could only know how much I love you, you would cry for joy!

---

1. Publisher's footnote:
    Though this request was generally followed by the press, it did not prohibit the Bishop of Mostar from issuing repeated attacks against Medjugorje, through the same press, and this, during the period of investigation by his Commission.

APPENDIX

THE ROLE OF OUR LADY
IN THE SALVATION OF MANKIND

God is incomprehensible and unattainable in His plans. This is clear to all of us. Innumerable times we have to marvel and wonder when we slowly discover, or perhaps only guess, what God has already materialized or will materialize in the history of the world and the Church.

The same is true about Our Lady, the Mother of the Son of God and Redeemer of the world. I am convinced that not one of us can even imagine all of Mary's greatness, given to her by God, and the entire role that God intended for her in the realization of His plans with mankind, through the history of the world and the Church.

God wanted it, but, no doubt Our Lady wished it herself (as a humble servant of the Lord) that she—though the Mother of the Redeemer—completely remain in the background in the life of her Son and during her life on earth after Christ's Ascension to Heaven. She also remained in the background in the Gospel, and in other books of the Holy Bible and during the long centuries of the history of the Church. But the Church slowly began to understand and acknowledge her place and her role. This understanding and accepting of the greatness of Our Lady is coming to its culmination.

The Church has not reached this summit, but I am convinced that the time is not far when the Church will reach it. The theologians, led and enlightened by the Spirit of God, have a big job ahead of them. But all of us, too, priests and faithful, must be engaged in this work, through our own contemplation, prayer and preaching, spreading the messages of Our Lady and expanding devotion to her. Thus we help and contribute to the realization of the final and complete triumph of Our Lady, that God wishes to give her, for our salvation and happiness. She announced this in Fatima when she said that her Immaculate Heart will triumph at the end.

In her apparitions in Amsterdam, as the "Lady of all Nations" (the apparitions started on March 25, 1945—the last ones were in 1981), Our Lady requested that the Church proclaim a dogma that she is the Co-Redeemer, Mediatrix, and Intercessor. In Marienfried (1946) she called herself the "Great Mediatrix of Grace." Perhaps, it will be just this acknowledgement of Our Lady's role in the very act of salvation, and of her role in distribution of the fruits of the redemption and the redeemed souls, that will represent the culmination that the Church must reach in comprehending and acknowledging the role of Mary.

It is certain that the apparitions of Our Lady in recent times, starting with Paris (1830) and La Salette (1846), have a special place. The theologians did not pay enough attention to these apparitions, in fact, so little attention, that they are hardly mentioned at all. I dare to state that it is a great omission of Catholic theology that will absolutely have to be addressed. If we think deeply about the messages of Our Lady during the apparitions, we discover a priceless wealth of ideas, incentives and graces, that will immensely enrich our religious and spiritual life and enable us to make great strides on our pilgrimage on the way to eternity.

I will mention here only one small thing: I was amazed by the humbleness that Our Lady displays during her apparitions. As if she completely forgets all the greatness that God has given her, she humbles herself and becomes only the lowly servant of God. As long ago in Nazareth, and in these her apparitions, she does only that which God in His plans conceived and ordered. Little Bernadette in Lourdes was amazed by the fact that Our Lady addressed her with "you" (plural form of courtesy in French). In other apparitions it differs since Our Lady always adapts to the mentality of the people, circumstances and situations of place and time. And something more. Bernadette's description of the vision on March 25, 1858, contains the statement that Bernadette, urged by an inner impulse, asked Our Lady three times: "Lady, be so kind, and tell me who you are." Bernadette explains:

"The Lady stood upright behind the wild rose bush and appeared to me in the way she is portrayed on the miraculous medal. When I asked her for the third time to tell me her name, her face became very serious; it seemed that she immersed into deep humility. She folded her hands, raised them and looked toward the sky. Then she extended her arms, leaned toward me and said with a trembling voice: *'I am the Immaculate Conception.'*"

With how much humility Our Lady admits her distinctive feature, the unique and unrepeated gift of God, her Immaculate Conception.

The final role that God intended for Our Lady in His plans for salvation of mankind, in the final phase of world history, we most certainly cannot know. We cannot even guess. But I am sure that this role will be extremely great, and it will surpass our most daring anticipations. Some reasons for it?

There can be no doubt that, of all God's creatures, including angels, Mary surrendered herself and offered herself to the disposition of her Creator, most readily, most perfectly, and with the greatest possible love of which any creature is capable. That happened from the first moment she became aware of herself and her Creator. God did not exempt any reasoning creature (except baptized infants who died) from temptation, neither human beings nor angels. Mary, too, most certainly had to experience, in some way, her temptation, but God did not reveal anything about it to us. We can only guess what went on in Mary's soul since her youth.

Michael the Archangel, immediately and from the first moment of temptation, decided for his Creator with all his being. (Lucifer was the first creation of God and the greatest of all angels, but also the great seducer who tried and succeeded in seducing many other angels from God.) Michael the Archangel has shown that no creature has the right to question

God's power over them. Therefore, we should not have any doubts that Mary, the future Queen and ruler of angels, decided for God with even a far greater love, readiness and surrender. God rewarded angels for their loyalty. Mary's reward is much greater, therefore her loyalty and love must have been much greater.

It is true that God gave Mary far greater gifts than to any other creature. But with her love and surrender she showed herself worthy of these gifts. With her perfect participation in the plan of God for the redeeming of mankind, she has completely justified the trust that God had shown her when He bestowed these gifts upon her. Thus, it is justified and well deserved that she was raised above all other creatures and, after being taken body and soul to Heaven, she has been crowned as Queen and ruler over all angels and men. However, Mary is not a Queen like earthly kings and rulers, for whom this is only an empty title with little power or true influence in politics and the destiny of their countries. Mary is a Queen with full power, and is a true Master of her subjects. She is the first, next to God.

In theology the principle is known and accepted that God does nothing or executes nothing by Himself if He can do it through His creatures. The bliss of Heaven (acknowledgment of the Divine Being) is not only some passive obtainment without any self activity. That blissful acknowledgment is indeed active, and requires the cooperation of all created beings, angels and men, equally. In this active inclusion all the fullness of joy is contained, all the bliss that a creature can achieve.

The relation to all other blessed in Heaven, angels and men, and to everything that has been created, is certainly extraordinarily active, and in this activity, the origin of many additional joys of eternal bliss can be found. As long as there are human beings on the earth, the activity of all the blessed in Heaven is extraordinarily great toward mankind and the Church on earth. The mystery of the Communion of Saints, the Communion of the Church on earth, the souls in Purgatory, and the blessed in Heaven is a powerful and unsurmised reality, about which our theology talks too little. It offers and extends to us as believers, an unimagined wealth of ideas and graces. Every creature—in Heaven and on the earth—has his completely separate and specific role which God intended only for him and which only he can accomplish.

According to God's plan and will, the greatest and most important role belongs to Mary, particularly in the realization of the salvation of mankind. Her role began when the Second Person (The Word) of God became Man. She gave the world the Redeemer, the Son of God. She offered Him to us even when she was standing under the Cross, when she was, according to God's will—Co-redeemer of mankind. She offers Him to us and mediates in Heaven, as the great Mediatrix of all graces that God distributes to us through the merits of Christ.

Fallen angels are the seducers in the temptation of man. Trial or temptation is something that God Himself wanted and which must inevitably happen to all reasonable beings because only the resisted temptation, the passed examination, enables us to achieve eternal bliss. Satan was given the possibility of influencing the destiny of the world and mankind. By the sins of people, Satan has obtained power and strength, that his influence could be such as it is today, fatal to all mankind and disastrous for all who—voluntarily through sin—give themselves to his power. The fight of Heaven and Hell, of God and Satan, takes place in man, in each individual, and in the whole community of mankind.

God Himself does not fight directly with Satan. He entrusted that fight to the angels—from the first shout of Michael the Archangel to the end of the world and mankind—and to the people here on earth where the fight exists for every individual. The souls in Heaven with their direct engagement—in a way—also act as co-redeemers and mediators and intercessors (by their prayers and merits). They also participate in that battle. And Our Lady is in that battle, as the Queen of Heaven and earth, the universe, the angels and all people. God entrusted to her the duty, honor and task to finally defeat Satan.

This her role, God announced in Paradise, immediately after the sin of the first man:

I will put enmity between you and the Woman, between your seed and her seed. He will crush your head and you will strike at His heel. (Gn. 3:15).

God announced here the hostility between Our Lady and Satan, and the "woman's offspring," her Son, Who will crush the head of Satan. But from other places in God's Revelation, it is clear that the Son of God executes that crushing of Satan's head through His mother. Through centuries, the Church used the Vulgata—the Latin translation of the Bible—where it was translated that she—the Woman—will crush the snake's head. This was an incorrect translation, but it was a translation that correctly expressed the belief of the Church and the intentions of God.

So it is in performing this her role, that through centuries of Church history, Our Lady progressed and reached culmination in our time. Through her apparitions, in a special way she directly and incomprehensibly, vividly engages in that human battle with the devil and with sin. When we observe the condition of the world today, it seems that Heaven was never as far from people on earth as it is today. However, observing the grasp of Our Lady on the destiny of mankind, we are forced to realize and acknowledge that Heaven was never—since the coming of the Holy Spirit—so close to the earth and mankind as it is today.

God does not abandon man. It is still true what we pray in the Fourth Canon of the Mass: "You have offered to people a covenant and instructed them through prophets to await salvation."

The role of prophets in the Old Testament, before the coming of Christ, is clear. But, in the New Testament, after the coming of Christ, prophesy still exists. The Church of Christ is built on the basis of the apostles and prophets, as St. Paul teaches (*Ep.* 2:30; 3:5). This does not mean just the prophets of the Old Testament, but various prophetic charisms of the New Testament as well.

In the decree of the Second Vatican Council regarding

charisms, it states: "Priests should discover them with feelings of faith, joyfully acknowledge them and cultivate them with care, so as not to extinguish the Spirit" (Lumen Gentium 9 and 12).

Specifically, according to St. Paul (*1 Th.* 5:19-210) *Never try to suppress the Spirit or treat the gift of prophecy with contempt; examine the accuracy of everything, and hold on to what is good.*

The Acts of the Apostles mention in several places prophetic charisms and the great influence and meaning of prophets in the beginning of the Church. On the initiative of the prophets, Paul and Barnabas were selected and sent to preach. In many places on the way to Jerusalem, the prophets told Paul what was awaiting him there.

This is then, a prophetic charism of the New Testament that God has given. He has been giving it through all the centuries, and gives it today to His Church, as an aid and complement to the regular leadership of the Church. Unfortunately, it is a fact that in the Church, throughout centuries, the meaning and importance of prophetic charism has been lost.

There were many causes and reasons for this and the human factor certainly played the main role. The prophetic charisms were often not accepted and this was many times a cause of damage to the Church. The human factor in the Church of God has gone farther today than ever before. If it does not directly deny the very possibility of God's supernatural involvement in the stream of history, it, to the extreme, avoids talking about it and simply does not concede even the possibility that God would still speak in this way today.

The greatest prophetic phenomenon of the New Testament is Our Lady herself. She is not only the Queen of Prophets, but, in a special way, a prophet in recent times in the Church and in the world. According to God's will and mission, Our Lady intervenes in the destiny of the world and mankind more than any of us can guess.

There have been more Marian apparitions in the world than those that we know of, and there are more apparitions today than ever before in history. Unfortunately, Our Lady, too, is experiencing the destiny of the prophets in that people do not listen to her, as they did not even listen to her Son but rejected Him and crucified Him. Most of the apparitions of Our Lady have not been acknowledged, often by the fault of the human factor in the Church. How many people there are, for example, who have not yet heard the word Fatima, or even worse, do not want to hear it, or reject it as a "private revelation."

In the light of these thoughts, we should observe Medjugorje and everything that is happening there, and particularly the messages that Our Lady is giving us. It is a fact that Medjugorje, by its duration, by the number of apparitions and messages and by their content, has surpassed all previous apparitions of Our Lady. I firmly believe that the apparitions in Medjugorje may not only be the last appearances of Our Lady on earth, but also the greatest, the crown of all her apparitions. We must pray that history does not repeat itself in that we not experience what the chosen people of God did long ago, when they did not recognize in Christ the promised Messiah, but rejected Him collectively and so lost the chance of their history.

In Medjugorje, Our Lady specifically gives us, through her weekly messages, and messages through the prayer groups, much more than she has ever before given through her apparitions. She resolutely leads us on the way of holiness. She is not satisfied that we become more or less good, average Christians and believers, but calls us more and more to holiness. In this way she is preparing an era of saints, a time when "her Immaculate Heart will triumph." It is up to us to obey the voice and the messages of our heavenly Mother, to follow them and to live as she wants us to live.

I also wish to call attention to the dogma about the Mystical Body of Christ which we all believe and accept, but which, unfortunately, has little influence in our everyday life. Christ said: *I am the vine, you are the branches. (Jn. 15:5).* With these words, He wanted to stress the bond of graces of all of us with Him; all of us who accept Him as our God and Saviour and who wish to follow Him.

St. Paul, a former persecutor of the Church of Christ, heard Christ's question: *Saul, Saul, why do you persecute me? (Acts 9:4-6)*. He realized that the faithful, Christ's followers, are the living and extended Christ. The root of his teaching is that Christ is the head, and we are the members of His Mystical Body.

Christ came to this world once, and through His suffering and death, He saved and sanctified the world and mankind. But He continues to live in His Church, in us and through us. He continues His work through His grace, through the action of the Holy Spirit. He lives and works and suffers in us and through us, and so in us and through us He will accomplish the salvation and sanctification of our brothers and sisters. He asks that we accept and live our roles in His Mystical Body.

In her messages, Our Lady wishes just that. We should be the living and conscious members of the Body of her Son. God selected "each one of us" for this, as Our Lady says in her message of January 25, 1987. She, too, is with us, so that we would be able to completely accomplish that plan. She is the Mother of Jesus and Mother of His Mystical Body, Mother of the Church, Queen of the prophets, teacher and guide on our journey toward eternity with God and Christ.

OUR LADY CONQUERS THE WORLD FOR CHRIST

As much as it would seem to somebody as being daring and arrogant, I wish to state two things:

Never before, in the entire history of mankind, as far as we know, after the Son of God walked in human form in this valley of tears, nor through the entire history of numerous and great mystics, Heaven has never come so close, so humanly and intimately close to mankind; close not only to the visionaries but to each one of us and to all people and mankind as now at Medjugorje.

Second: It is certain that not one of us is even able to guess the greatness and importance, significance and power that God's mercy has ignited by the coming of Our Lady to Medjugorje.

I am deeply convinced that Our Lady came down to the dry and waterless chalky rocks of Hercegovina and that in spite of everything—in this our time of defection from God and Church—remains, in the greatest part, an oasis of faith in the desert of modern godlessness and diluted and impoverished Christianity. She came so that from there a torrent of a general renewal would begin to flow and soon transform Hercegovina and the whole country, all of Europe, and finally the whole world, into a rich and blooming Kingdom of God. Then all the biblical prophecies, not yet fulfilled, will be finally realized about the messianic Kingdom of Christ and the prophecy of Our Lady at Fatima that her Immaculate Heart will finally win and celebrate her triumph.

In Medjugorje, Our Lady finally stepped into her conquering and victorious visitation that she has been preparing for a long time through her various apparitions, starting with Paris (Miraculous Medal, 1830), La Salette (1846), Lourdes (1858), Fatima (1917) and many other places of her appearances (especially after the last war) to conquer the world for Christ.

Since other apparitions of Our Lady are not well known, I am adding here a short description, with at least the most important facts of the apparitions.

PARIS, 1830

Catherine Labouré was born as one of many children in the family of a farmer. When she was 9 years old, she lost her mother and since then was in a special way devoted to the Virgin Mary: "You will be my Mother now!" At the age of 24, she joined the religious order of the Sisters of Mercy of St. Vincent de Paul and in June 1830 began her novitiate in the Motherhouse in Paris.

Our Lady appeared to her two times. The first time was during the night of July 19-20, 1830 in the chapel of the Motherhouse. Mary told her:

"There are difficult times now. France will be afflicted by misfortunes. The throne will fall. In the whole world, calamities will bring riots...The Cross will be abused and thrown to the ground; they will pierce again the Heart of Our Lord. Blood will flow in the streets; the whole world will be immersed in sadness..."

"Come in front of this altar; here, graces will be poured for all people who pray for them, great and small...Have confidence; do not be discouraged; I will be with you!"

Our Lady told her to tell her confessor everything. "He, who will soon become the superior, should work diligently that the lives of both religious orders of St. Vincent de Paul—the Lazarists and the Sisters of Mercy—be renewed in the spirit of rules, because those orders had become lukewarm in many things."

The second apparition was on Saturday, on the eve of the first Sunday of Advent, November 27, 1830, in the same chapel, while the sisters contemplated the rules of their order. Our Lady appeared standing on a hemisphere; in her hand she carried a smaller sphere, the globe. On the hands of Our Lady were rings with precious stones. The globe disappeared from her hands and from the precious stones came a kind of fire that was prolonged into rays. Our Lady lowered and spread her arms and the rays fell on the hemisphere on which Our Lady was standing.

Catherine heard a voice: "This sphere represents the whole world, particularly France, and every man separately. The rays of light are symbols of the graces that Our Lady pours on those who pray for them."

Then, an oval wreath appeared around Our Lady. In the wreath was written with golden letters: *O Mary, conceived without sin, pray for us who have recourse to you.* Then the picture turned around and Catherine saw the other side of the oval. In the center was the capital letter M into which a cross was wedged. Under the letter were two hearts: One with a wreath of thorns, the other pierced by a sword. Around everything was a wreath of stars. Then Catherine heard the voice:

"Let them make a medal, according ot this model. All who will wear it, will receive great graces. The graces will be very rich for those who will wear the medal with trust."

Great misfortunes came to France after 40 years, as Catherine foretold it. The confessor accepted Catherine with some doubts, but was quickly convinced that the vision was true when some events happened that Our Lady had announced. Both religious orders of St. Vincent de Paul were renewed to the previous principles and according to the rule of the Founder. By the permission of the bishop, in the year 1832, the first medals were made which soon became known as "Miraculous Medals" because of great graces, many healings and conversions for persons who wore them. They were soon known and used throughout the whole world.

At that time, the dogma about the Immaculate Conception was not yet announced. That happened 24 years later, in the year 1854.

Except to her confessor, Catherine did not tell anybody about her visions. He made them known publicly, but did not reveal the name of the seer. He mentioned only that the seer is one of the Sisters of Mercy. Catherine later lived in Paris, taking care of the old and sick for 40 years. She was very popular, but as a seer completely unknown. Only shortly before her death, 1876, after her confessor was dead for a long time, Catherine did tell the whole story to her Superior. She was pronounced a saint in 1947.

By these apparitions Our Lady wished to:

- Renew the orders of the Lazarists and the Sisters of Mercy;
- Invite people to trust in her, the Virgin conceived without sin. The symbol of this trust is the wearing of the "Miraculous Medal";
- Call people to turn to Jesus in their troubles and needs; He is permanently present in the tabernacles of our churches;
- Give the initiative to organize the society "Children of Mary" that soon spread around the world and is similar to the Congregation of Mary.

For His great deeds, God regularly selects tiny and insignificant tools and persons. It was the same here. Through the insignificant and unknown sister Catherine Labouré and the Miraculous Medal, Mary began, according to God's will, her great enterprise of conquering the world for Christ, the enterprise that would continue in other apparitions.

LA SALETTE, 1846

La Sallette is located in the southeast of France, high in the Alps. There were two seers: Maximin Giraud and and Mélanie Calvat. Maximin was a little over 11 years old and Mélanie was 15, but looked like she was only 12 years old. Both were children of poor farmer families, without any schooling; uneducated in religion—they could hardly say the Our Father. They had to go to work early; they took care of the cows on mountain pastures for rich farmers. Only in winter months did they stay home. Though they were from the same village, they did not know each other until the day before the apparition. And on that day they found themselves "by chance" in the pasture with the cows.

September 19, 1846 was an ember-day Saturday and the eve of the feast day of the Lady of Seven Sorrows. Around 2:30 P.M. in the afternoon, both of them noticed a shiny "beautiful lady" who was weeping throughout the entire apparition. She said to them:

"If my people do not convert, I have to let my Son's arm fall. It is so heavy that I cannot hold it up anymore...I have suffered already so long for you."

Our Lady complained particularly about the sin of neglecting the Sunday as the Lord's Day and about the sin of cursing that insults the name of her Son.

"You must pray in the morning and in the evening. If you do not know more, pray at least the Our Father and the Hail Mary. When you have time, you must pray more.

"There are only a few old women who come to Holy Mass. The others work on Sunday throughout the whole summer, and in the winter. When they do not have anything else to do, they come to the Holy Mass and make fun of religion."

Our Lady had announced many misfortunes that would happen to France because of the sins by which God is offended:

plant diseases will ruin wheat and potatoes, nuts and vineyards. People will die from hunger and illnesses, especially children under seven years of age.

When leaving, Our Lady also said: "My children, tell that to all the people!"

Our Lady appeared only once. Whatever she had announced, was fulfilled. The plant disease ruined potatoes and wheat in France and in other countries. In the year 1851, vineyards suffered from the before unknown disease (peronospora) which spread through the whole of Europe. In the year 1852, disease ruined the nuts. In the years 1854 and 1855, over 150,000 people died from hunger and in the year 1864 just as many from cholera, and half of this number were children under seven years of age. Then came the war 1870-71 with its horrors.

Our Lady had given each one of the seers one secret. Mélanie told her secret to Pope Pius IX who said that the meaning of that secret corresponds with the words of Jesus: *If you do not convert, you will all perish!* (*Lk.* 13:5).

The bishop of the diocese Grenoble, to which La Salette belongs, acknowledged the verity of the apparitions on September 19, 1851, after the commission that he established gave a positive judgment about the apparition.

LOURDES, 1858

Lourdes is a small city on the south-southwest of France, under the mountain of Pyrenees. Marie Bernards (Bernadette) Soubirous, was born on February 17, 1844 in Lourdes, as the oldest of six children. Her father was a miller, mostly without work. They lived in extreme poverty. In the year 1858, they lived in a former jail, a narrow and damp apartment where Bernadette, in poor health since childhood, became sick with asthma from which she suffered all her life.

Because of poverty and because she had to help her mother with her younger brothers, she hardly attended school. She was very poorly instructed about religion, but learned early in her life to pray the rosary that she prayed with joy every day. During the winter of 1858, she attended school more regularly at the school of nuns and was preparing for her first holy communion.

During the time of February 11 to July 7, 1858 Our Lady appeared to Bernadette 18 times. All the apparitions were in the grotto Massabielle next to the river Gave, a little lower than Lourdes.

During the apparition on February 18, Our Lady made a promise to Bernadette: "I do not promise to make you happy in this world, but in the other. . ." On February 21 she said: "Pray for sinners!" On February 25, in the grotto, after Mary's words, "Go, drink and wash yourself at the spring," water started to flow from a spring that was not there before and that has not dried up to this day. The water from this spring, of course with prayer and intercession from the Mother of God, has healed many ill persons.

On February 26, Our Lady said, "Penance, penance, penance." Bernadette later said, "Our Lady told me that I must pray and do penance for sinners." On March 2, Our Lady said, "Go to the priests and tell them to build a chapel here and to come here in processions." On March 25, after repeated requests from Bernadette, Mary told her name: *I am the Immaculate Conception.*

In the beginning, the priests took not only a very reserved position toward the apparitions, but they were opposed to accepting them and acted even hostile toward them. The bishop from Tarbes established a commission that examined everything very thoroughly. In his pastoral letter from January 18, 1862, he stated:

"According to our judgment, the Mother of God, conceived without sin, truly appeared to Bernadette Soubirous on February 11, 1858 and some days after that, in the grotto Massabielle, close to the city of Lourdes. These apparitions contain signs of the truth and it has been allowed for the faithful to consider them truthful."

Above the grotto Massabielle, a magnificent basilica was built. Lourdes has become the greatest pilgrimage place of universal proportions and pilgrims come there from the whole world.

Bernadette received her first Holy Communion on July 3, 1858 in the chapel of the nuns in Lourdes. After that, she had only one more vision, the last vision. On July 4, 1866 she left Lourdes and said goodbye to the grotto. She went to Nevers, where on July 29 she became a novice at the same order of sisters who were her teachers in Lourdes. She suffered much from her illness, and died young, on April 16, 1879 in Nevers. She said about herself: "A broom is needed to clean the house, and after that, it is put behind the door." She was proclaimed a saint in 1933.

The main purpose of the apparitions in Lourdes was evidently the statement of Our Lady, *I am the Immaculate Conception,* which acknowledged the dogma about her Immaculate Conception which was proclaimed by Pope Pius IX on December 8, 1854. In addition, Our Lady repeated the call to penance and conversion that she had given also at La Salette.

FATIMA, 1917

Fatima is a village in the geographical center of Portugal, about half-way between Lisbon at the south and Coimbre at the north, in a mountainous rocky region. The land is poor and the people are poor, but they were, in general, good and faithful, at least at that time. That was during the first World War. Portugal was in the war on the side of France and England.

There were three visionaries: Lucy dos Santos who at the beginning of the apparitions was a little over 10 years of age, her cousin Francisco Marto, about 9 years old, and his sister Jacinta, a little more than seven years old. All three were from the village Aljustrel, close to Fatima which has a parish church consecrated to St. Anthony. All three were shepherds; they took care of sheep.

In the year 1916 (the children did not know the date) they had a vision of an angel three times who said that he was the angel of peace and the angel of Portugal. He invited them to pray and make sacrifices for peace, as a reparation for sins and for the conversion of sinners. The angel had taught them a prayer and asked them to pray it often. The first part of the prayer he taught them at the first apparition, and the second part at the third apparition:

My God, I believe in You, I adore You, I trust You and I love You! I beg of You to forgive those who do not believe, who do not adore You, who do not trust You and who do not love You.

Most Holy Trinity, Father, Son and Holy Spirit, I offer you the Body, Blood, Soul and Divinity of Jesus Christ, present in all the tabernacles of the world, as a reparation for the outrages, sacrileges and indifferences by which He is offended. By the infinite merits of the Sacred Heart of Jesus and the Immaculate Heart of Mary, I beg the conversion of poor sinners.

During the year 1917, Our Lady appeared to the children six times, from May 13 to October 13; always on the 13th day of the month in Cova da Iria, a valley about two and a half kilometers from Aljusrel. Only in August, the apparition occurred on the 19th of August in the place called Valinhos, not far from their village, because on the 13th of August, the children were in jail.

During the first apparition, on May 13, Our Lady asked them: *Do you want to offer God all the sufferings He will send you, as a reparation for sins that have offended God and to obtain the conversion of sinners?* "Yes, we will," answered the children. Our Lady also invited them to pray the rosary every day "to obtain peace by prayer."

Our Lady repeated the call to pray the rosary at every apparition.

During the second apparition, on June 13, Our Lady said that she would soon take to her Francisco and Jacinta, but that Lucy must remain. Jesus wants her to serve Him and to establish devotion to the Immaculate Heart of Mary in the world.

To those who will persevere in this devotion, I promise salvation. God will especially love those souls, and they will be as flowers, an adornment to His Throne! Then she said to Lucy: *Do not be discouraged; I will never leave you. My Immaculate Heart will be your protection and the way with which I will lead you to God.*

Then Our Lady showed them her Immaculate Heart that became visible in a circle of light, encircled by a wreath of thorns. The children understood that this was her immaculate heart and that the wreath of thorns signified offenses accumulated on it and that she had shown it to them as an incentive for prayer and penance.

During the third apparition, on July 13, Our Lady announced that in October she would perform a great miracle so that everyone would believe. Then she said: *Make sacrifices for sinners and pray this prayer often when you make a sacrifice:*

O my Jesus, this is for the love of You, for conversion of sinners and as reparation for offenses committed against the Immaculate Heart of Mary.

After that she told the children the famous secret of Fatima that has three parts. Lucy later revealed the first two parts, and the third one she wrote down and, through the bishop, she sent it to the pope, but that part has not yet been revealed.

The first part of the secret was a vision of Hell. In the second part, Our Lady said: *You saw Hell where the souls of the poor sinners go. To save them, God wishes to establish in the world a devotion to my Immaculate Heart. If people accept what I am saying, many souls will be saved and peace will come. The war is ending. But if people do not stop offending God, during the pontificate of Pius XI, another war will start, a worse war. . .To prevent it, I will ask for the consecration of Russia to my Immaculate Heart and as a retribution, Holy Communion on the five consecutive first Saturdays in a month. If people accept my requests, Russia will be converted and there will be peace. If they do not accept them, Russia will spread fallacies in the world and will provoke wars and persecution of the Church. Good people will be persecuted; the Holy Father will suffer much; various nations will be destroyed. Finally, my Heart will triumph. The Holy Father will consecrate Russia to me, and it will be converted and the world will be given a period of peace... When you are say-ing the rosary, say after each decade: "O my Jesus, forgive us our sins, save us from the fires of Hell; lead all souls to Heaven, especially those in most need of your mercy!"*

During the fourth apparition, on August 19, the Mother of God sent this message: *Pray, pray much, and make sacrifices for sinners. You must know that many souls go to Hell be-cause nobody prays for them nor makes sacrifices for them.*

During the fifth apparition, September 13, Our Lady repeated her promise that she would perform a miracle on October 13.

October 13 was the sixth and the last apparition. Our Lady said: *I am the Lady of the Holy Rosary... Mankind should not offend Our Lord anymore, because He is already too much offended!* Then the children saw St. Joseph and the boy Jesus beside Our Lady; they saw Jesus as he blessed the people, then they saw Our Lady of the Seven Sorrows and then Our Lady of Carmel.

Persons who were present at that time, experienced an un-usual miracle; a strange and unexplainable dance of the sun that could be seen for miles away and that lasted about ten minutes. People were all wet from rain and dirty from mud through which they walked, but after that miracle, they saw that their clothes were completely dry.

Before Christmas in 1918, Francisco and Jacinta became ill with "Spanish" influenza, epidemics that ravaged through Eu-rope after the first World War. Both suffered much, but both accepted and endured the illness with heroic resignation and patience and offered their suffering for the intentions that Our Lady suggested to them. Before her death, Jacinta often saw Our Lady. Francisco died on April 4, 1919, and Jacinta on February 20, 1920.

In 1925 Lucy joined the order of the Sisters of St. Dorotz in Pontevedra in Spain. She moved to the Carmelite convent in Coimbri in Portugal, where she still lives today. In the year 1926, the boy Jesus appeared to her and requested that she announce and spread the devotion to the Immaculate Heart of Mary. Our Lady appeared to her several times; in the year

1929 she told her to request the consecration of Russia to the Immaculate Heart of Mary.

At the time of the apparitions, Fatima belonged to the patriarchy of Lisbon. It was in the year 1920 that the diocese of Leiria was established. The Bishop of Leiria then established a commission that worked for seven years on the examination of the apparitions. The Bishop of Leiria acknowledged the truthfulness of the apparitions of Fatima on October 13, 1930 and approved devotion to Our Lady of Fatima.

A WORD OR TWO MORE...

In addition to those apparitions of Our Lady, there were several other apparitions in Europe in the time before the second World War, but the ones described here are the most significant. The apparitions in Fatima are definitely the most important. If the Church were not that slow in acknowledging their truthfulness, if the bishops, priests and the faithful took them more seriously and accepted the messages of Our Lady, particularly the ones about conversion, praying the rosary and devotion to the Immaculate Heart of Mary, the history of the world and mankind would have probably turned in a different direction.

It is unbelievable that it took a full quarter of a century for Europe to learn about Fatima, in spite of the fact that Portugal is in Europe, though at her border. Only in the midst of the second World War and its horror, the messages spread throughout the world about the Fatima apparitions and messages. After the last war, devotion to the Immaculate Heart of Mary and the devotion of five first Saturdays became quite well known, but not well enough. The messages of Our Lady were still very little known.

At the middle of the sixties, an otherwise good and reputable priest told me: "The Church must be defatimized!" (That means be freed from the messages from Fatima and their influence). He did not understand their significance and importance.

"Defatimization" unfortunately spread quickly and thoroughly, and Fatima is today practically forgotten, along with devotion to the Immaculate Heart of Mary and the devotion of five first Saturdays. Instead of a renewal in faith and Christian life, the Church passes through and experiences a time of great defection, as never before in history.

After the last war, among numerous apparitions of Our Lady in the world, particularly in Europe, there are some that seem to be truthful and very important for the entire Church and the world, but the human factor in God's Church has succeeded in thwarting God's intentions. If it were different, Medjugorje probably would not be necessary.

And then came Medjugorje. God has shown that He is persevering, indeed, "obstinately" persevering, in His love toward unfortunate and sinful mankind, and that He cannot be distracted by unbelief and rejection. In spite of the contrary mood in the Church among many theologians and faithful, who feel every direct influence of God as actually repulsive, God finds ways to break through all of this and overcomes the obstacles by creating conditions and opportunities so that no human power can nor will destroy His work or thwart His plans any longer. The Church and mankind are confronted with a dilemma: to acknowledge and accept Our Lady and her messages that she directs to us in the name of God and be saved, or to "thwart" God's intentions with inestimable damage for themselves, for the whole Church and all of mankind.

John the Baptist shouted to his contemporaries: *The axe is already placed down on the roots of the trees.* (*Mt.* 3:12; *Lk.* 3:9).

Our Lady of Medjugorje, the Queen of Peace, begs for our nation and the entire Church and all of mankind to receive the light and the grace of the Holy Spirit, that they understand the signs of the time, that they accept the offered grace to return to their God and that they find in Him happiness, joy and peace!

PRAYERS

A Cry

O God, our heart is in deep darkness, In spite of this it is bound to Your Heart.

Our heart struggles between You and Satan; do not allow this to be!

And every time our heart is divided between good and evil, may it be illuminated by Your light and made whole.

Never allow two loves to dwell within us, or that two faiths may ever co-exist; never allow to dwell amongst us:

Falsehood and sincerity, love and hate, honesty and dishonesty, humility and pride.

Rather, help us so that our heart may rise up to You like that of a child.

Let our heart be captured by peace and may it ever continue to feel a longing for peace.

May Your holy will and Your love find their abode in us, that at least sometimes we desire truly to be Your children.

And when, Lord, we do not wish to be Your children, remember our past desires and help us to receive You once more.

We open our hearts to You so that Your holy love may dwell in them;

We open our souls to You so that they may be touched by Your holy mercy, which will help us to see all our sins clearly and will make us understand that what renders us impure is sin!

O God, we wish to be Your children, so humble and devoted, and through this to become dear and sincere children, as only the Father could wish us to be.

Help us, Jesus, our brother, that Your Father be good to us and help us to be good toward Him.

Help us, Jesus, to understand clearly the good that God gives us, because sometimes we give up doing a good deed, believing it to be a wrong."

(After this prayer, recite the Glory Be three times.)
(June 22, 1985)

Consecration to the Immaculate Heart of Mary

O Immaculate Heart of Mary, ardent with goodness, show

your love toward us.

May the flame of Your Heart, O Mary, descend on all mankind.

We love you immensely.

Impress true love in our hearts so that we have a continuous desire for you.

O Mary, meek and humble of heart, remember us when we are in sin.

Give us, by means of your Immaculate and Motherly Heart, spiritual health.

Let us always see the goodness of your Maternal Heart.

May we be converted by means of the flame of your Heart. Amen.

(November 28, 1983)

Consecration to the Sacred Heart of Jesus

O Merciful Jesus, You offered us Your Heart.

It is crowned with thorns and with our sins.

You constantly implore us not to go astray.

Jesus, be merciful to us when we are in sin.

By means of Your Heart make all people love one another.

Make hate disappear among mankind.

Show us Your love.

We love You and want You to protect us with Your Shepherd's Heart; from us from every sin.

Jesus, enter into every heart.

Knock, knock at the door of our hearts.

Be patient and never desist.

We are still closed because we have not understood Your love.

Knock continuously.

O good Jesus, make us open our hearts to You, especially when we remember Your Passion suffered for us. Amen.

(November 28, 1983)

Prayer for the Sick

O my God, this sick person here before You has come to

ask You what he desires, and what he believes to be the most important thing for himself.

Grant, O God, that these words enter into his heart:

"It is important to be healthy in the soul!"

Lord, may Your holy will be done unto him in everything. If you wish that he be healed, may he be given health.

But if Your will is different, may he continue to bear his cross. I pray to You also for us who intercede for him:

Purify our hearts so as to make us worthy for Your holy mercy to be given through us.

Protect him and relieve his sufferings, may Your holy will be done unto him.

Through him may Your holy love be revealed; help him bear his cross with courage.

(After this prayer, recite the Glory Be three times.)

(June 22, 1985)

SOURCES AND BIBLIOGRAPHY

Personal observations, conversations with the visionaries, witnesses and pilgrims.

Schematism of the Franciscan province of Herzegovina from year 1977 (Croatian)

Anthology *Krsni Zavicaj* (Rocky Land), Numbers 14 to 19, year 1981-86. In every issue is a special supplement about Medjugorje. (Croatian)

Articles, issued periodically about Medjugorje, in *Glas Koncila* (Voice of the Council), *Nasa Ognjista* (Our Hearts), *Sveta Bastina* (Sacred Heritage), and other religious and nonreligious publications. (Croatian)

Reports and articles of Franciscans in Medjugorje, reproduced and sent to friends. (Croatian)

Dr. LJUDEVIT RUPCIC, *Gospina ukazanja u Medjugorju* (Apparitions of Our Lady in Medjugorje), 1983 (Croatian)

JANKO BUBALO, *Tisucu susreta s Gospom u Medjugorju* (A Thousand Meetings with Our Lady in Medjugorje), Jelsa 1985 (Croatian)

Prof. H. JOYEUX—Abbé R. LAURENTIN, *Scientific and Medical Studies on the Apparitions at Medjugorje,* 1987 (English)

ARMAND GIRARD—GUY GIRARD—JANKO BUBALO, *Medjugorje—Blagoslovljena zemlja—Svjedocanstva,* (Medjugorje—Blessed Land—Testimonies), Jelsa 1986 (Croatian)

Poruke mira—Medjugorje (Messages of Peace—Medjugorje), 3rd edition, Zagreb 1986 (Croatian)

Poruke mira—Medjugorje (Messages of Peace), No. 2, Zagreb 1986 (Croatian)

Poruke mira—Medjugorje (Messages of Peace), No. 3 (but number not indicated), Duvno 1987 (Croatian)

Gospine poruke—Medjugorje (Messages of Our Lady), Sveta Bastina, Duvno, 1987 (Croatian)

FRANZ HUMMER—CHRISTIAN JUNGWIRTH, *Medjugorje, Izyjesca-Slike-Dokumenti,* (Medjugorje, Reports—Pictures—Documents), Sveta Rastina, Duvno 1986 (Croatian)

Articles about Medjugorje published periodically in religious

and nonreligious publications in German-speaking countries.
R. LAURENTIN—L. RUPCIC, *Das Geschehen von Medjugorje, eine Untersuchung* (Events in Medjugorje, an Analysis), published by Styria, Graz, 1985 (German)
KURT KNOTZINGER, *Antwort Auf Medjugorje* (Answer to Medjugorje), Published by Styria Graf 1985. (German)
JOSEF GOUBERT—L. CRISTIANI, *Marienerscheinungen* (Apparitions of Mary), published by Paulus Verlag, Recklighausen, 1955 (German)
PETER MANNS, Reformer der Kirche, (Reformer of the Church), published by Matthias Grünewald Verlag, Mainz, 1970 (German)
JOHANNES MARIA HÖCHT, *Die grosse Botschaft von La Salette* (The Great Message from La Salette), published by Christiana Verlag, Stein am Rhein, 5th edition, 1983 (German)
YVES IVONIDES, *Fatima, da ili ne,* (Fatima, Yes or No), Zagreb 1977 (Croatian)

THE RIEHLE FOUNDATION

The Riehle Foundation is a non-profit, tax-exempt ministry dedicated to the Mother of God and her role in the salvation of mankind. It exists to produce and distribute spiritual books and materials to anyone, anywhere.

The Foundation publishes additional books on Medjugorje, including the works of Fr. René Laurentin. For additional information, or book availability, contact the Riehle Foundation.

All donations for books, though not required, are deeply appreciated, and are used for the printing and distribution of this material. We enlist your prayers and support.

The Riehle Foundation
P.O. Box 7
Milford, OH 45150